T̶H̶E̶ ̶A̶R̶M̶Y̶

W9-AOC-327

POCKET GUIDE

1997/ 1998

Editor - Charles Heyman

Copyright © R & F (Military Publishing) 1997

ISBN 0 85052 539 X

First Edition 1984
Second Edition 1987
Third Edition 1991
Fourth Edition 1993
Fifth Edition 1995
Sixth Edition 1997

Price £4.95 (Mail Order £5.25)

This edition published by

Pen & Sword Books Ltd
47 Church Street
Barnsley S70 2AS

Telephone : 01226 734222   Fax : 01226 734438

The information in this publication has been gathered from unclassified sources.

Front Cover: 155mm AS 90 of 1 RHA on route to gun positions in Bosnia during late 1996.
Rear Cover: A soldier of 1 RWF during an exercise on Salisbury Plain during mid 1996.

CONTENTS

Chapter 12 - Recruiting

Chapter 13 Reserve Forces

Chapter 14 - Miscellaneous

CHAPTER 1 - OVERVIEW

General Information

Populations - European Union Top Five Nations
(1995 estimates)

Germany	81.7 million
United Kingdom	58.6 million
France	58.1 million
Italy	57.7 million
Spain	39.1 million

Finance - European Union Top Five Nations
(1995 figures)

	GDP		Per Capita Income
Germany	DM3,035 bn	(US$1,908 bn)	US$22,100
France	Ff7,677 bn	(US$1, 538 bn)	US$20,700
United Kingdom	700 bn	(US$1,104 bn)	US$18,600
Italy	L1,769 tr	(US$1,069 bn)	US$19,300
Spain	P69,722 bn	(US$559 bn)	US$14,500

UK Population

England	-	47,055,204
Wales	-	2,835,073
Scotland	-	4,998,567
Northern Ireland	-	1,573,282
Total	-	56,462,166

Figures are from the 1991 census. The population split in Northern Ireland is approximately 56% Protestant and 41% Roman Catholic with the remaining 3% not falling into either classification. The latest (1995) estimate is that the overall population was approximately 58.6 million.

UK Population - Breakdown Military Service Groups

Age Group:	13-17	18-22	23-32
Men	1,819,000	1,883,000	4,489,000
Women	1,731,000	1,794,000	4,322,000

UK Area
(in square kilometres)

England	-	130,423
Wales	-	20,766
Scotland	-	77,167
Northern Ireland	-	14,121
Total	-	242,477

UK Government

The executive government is vested nominally in the Crown, but for practical purposes in a committee of Ministers that is known as the Cabinet. The head of the ministry and leader of the Cabinet is the Prime Minister. For the implementation of policy the Cabinet is dependent upon the support of a majority of the Members of Parliament in the House of Commons. Within the Cabinet defence matters are the responsibility of the Secretary of State for Defence.

UNITED KINGDOM DEFENCE OVERVIEW

Total British Armed Forces (as at 1 April 1996)

Regular: 222,300; Locally Entered 4,800; Regular Reserves 263,800; Volunteer Reserves 63,400; Cadet Forces 133,000; MOD Civilians 126,700 (of which 109,900 are employed in the UK).

Regular Army 112,000; Royal Navy 48,300; Royal Air Force 64,700; (Note: Royal Naval figure includes some 6,918 Royal Marines.

Forecast strengths for 1 April 1997 are: Army 111,000; Royal Navy 46,000 Royal Air Force 57,000 (following redundancy programme).

Strategic Forces: 3 x Vanguard Class submarines (SSBN ballistic missile submarine nuclear fuelled) with 16 x Trident D5 submarine launched ballistic missiles (SLBM). A fourth Vanguard Class submarine will probably become operational in 1998. Each submarine deploys with 96 x A90 MIRV warheads (multiple independently targeted re-entry vehicles) with probably six of these warheads on each missile.

Royal Navy: 48,300: 3 x SSBN; 12 x Submarines; 3 x Aircraft Carriers; 36 x Destroyers and Frigates; 18 x Mine Counter Measures Vessels; 8 x Offshore Patrol Craft; 27 x Coastal Patrol Craft; 1 x Ice Patrol Ship; 6 x Survey Vessels; 4 x Harrier Squadrons; 14 x Helicopter Squadrons; 3 x Royal Marines Commando Groups: Royal Fleet Auxiliary - 2 x Large Fleet Tankers; 3 x Small Fleet Tankers; 4 x Support Tankers; 5 x Fleet Replenishment Ships; 1 x Aviation Training Ship; 4 x Landing Ships; 1 x Forward Repair Ship.

Merchant Navy: Merchant Naval Vessels Registered in the UK and Crown Dependencies: 106 x Tankers (2161); 22 x Bulk Carriers (293); 13 x Specialised Carriers (124) ; 26 x Cellular Container Ships (1017); 86 x RoRo Passenger and Cargo Ships (657) ; 82 x Other General Cargo Ships (145); 9 x Passenger Ships (272); 69 x Tugs.

Note: This listing refers to vessels of 500 gross tons and over. The figures in brackets refer to thousands of gross tons relating to each type of vessel. The total is 4,670 thousand gross tons.

Air Force: 64,700; 6 x Strike/Attack Squadrons with 72 x Tornado GR1; 5 x Offensive Support Squadrons with 45 x Harrier GR7/T10 and 24 x Jaguar GR1A/B; 6 x Air Defence Squadrons with 80 x Tornado F3; 3 x Maritime Patrol Squadrons with 21 x Nimrod MR2; 5 x Reconnaissance Squadrons with 24 x Tornado GR1A, 1 x Jaguar T2A, 2 x Nimrod R1 and 5 x Canberra; 2 x Airborne Early Warning Squadrons with 7 x AEW Sentry; 17 x Transport, Tanker and Helicopter Squadrons with 10 x VC10 C1K, 9 x Tristar, 49 x Hercules, 27 x Chinook, 32 x Puma, 36 x Wessex, 15 x VC10 Tankers ; 2 x Search and Rescue Squadrons with 16 x Sea King HAR3; 6 x Surface to Air Missile Squadrons; 5 x Ground Defence Squadrons.

Army: 112,000 (including some 4,480 Gurkhas); 1 x Corps Headquarters in Germany (ARRC); 1 x Armoured Divisional HQ in Germany; 1 x Mechanised Divisional HQ in UK ; 3 x Brigade Headquarters in Germany; 17 x Brigade Headquarters in UK.

British Army Major Units

(at 1 Jan 1996)	Germany	UK	Elsewhere	TA
Armoured Regts	6	3	-	-
Armoured Recce Regts	1	1	-	5
Armoured Infantry Bns	6	2	-	-
Mechanised Bns	-	4	-	-
Airmobile Bns	-	2	-	-
Parachute Bns	-	3	-	2
Light Role Bns	-	19	2	34
Gurkha Bns	-	1	1	-
Total Infantry (1)	6	31	3	36
Army Air Corps Regiments	1	4	-	1
Artillery Field Regts	4	8	-	3
Air Defence Regts	2	2	-	3
Engineer Regiments	4	6	-	9
Signals Regiments	3	6	2	11
EW Regiment	1	-	-	-
Equipment Support Bns	3	2	-	5
Logistic Regiments	9	15	2	11
Fd Ambulances/Hospitals	3	9	-	18

Note (1) Excludes the 6 x Home Service Battalions of the Royal Irish Regiment and 1 x Battalion of the Gibraltar Regiment.

British Army Equipment Summary

Armour: 379 x Challenger 1 - 386 Challenger 2 on order; 104 x Sabre (approx); 88 x Striker; 300 x Scimitar; 1,600 x Fv 432; 789 x MCV 80 Warrior; 400 x Spartan; 655 x Saxon.
Awaiting Disposal - Approx 350 x Chieftain; 200 x Scorpion.

Artillery: 500 x 81mm Mortar; 2093 x 51mm Light Mortar; 179 x AS 90; 62 x 227mm MLRS; 36 x FH 70; 72 x 105mm Light Gun.

Air Defence: 40 x Rapier Fire Units; 382 x Javelin Launchers; 135 x Starstreak HVM.

Army Aviation: 126 x Lynx ; 159 Gazelle; 7 x BN-2; 7 x DHC2 and 21 Chipmunk (for training). Helicopters available from RAF- 32 x Chinook; 54 x Wessex; 37 x Puma; 67 x Longbow Apache on order.

Defence Roles and Responsibilities

The aim of the United Kingdom's Armed Forces is to deliver and sustain an operational capability wherever and whenever it is required. This overall aim is translated into the three major National Defence Roles.

Defence Role 1 - To ensure the protection and security of the United Kingdom and its dependent territories, even when there is no major external threat.
Defence Role 2 - To ensure against any major external threat to the United Kingdom and its allies.
Defence Role 3 - To contribute towards promoting the United Kingdom's wider security interests through the maintenance of international peace and stability.

These three Defence Roles are further subdivided into a number of Military Tasks (MT) which accurately define the way in which these Defence Roles are actually accomplished.

Ministry of Defence (MoD)

In 1963 the three independent service ministries were merged to form the present Ministry of Defence (MoD). This massive organisation which directly affects the lives of about half a million servicemen, reservists and MoD employed civilians, is controlled by The Secretary of State for Defence who is assisted by two ministers. The first of these is the Minister of State for the Armed Forces and the second the Minister of State for Defence Procurement.

The Secretary of State for Defence chairs The Defence Council. This Defence Council is the body that makes the policy decisions that ensure the three services are run efficiently, and in accordance with the wishes of the government of the day.

Defence Council

The composition of The Defence Council is as follows

The Secretary of State for Defence
Minister of State (Armed Forces)
Minister of State (Defence Procurement)
Parliamentary Under-Secretary of State for the Armed Force
Chief Scientific Adviser
Chief of Defence Procurement
Chief of Personnel & Logistics
Chief of the Defence Staff
Vice-Chief of the Defence Staff
Chief of the Naval Staff and First Sea Lord
Chief of the Air Staff
Chief of the General Staff
Second Permanent Under Secretary of State

Chief of The Defence Staff

The Chief of the Defence Staff (CDS) is the officer responsible to the Secretary of State for

Defence for the coordinated effort of all three fighting services. He has his own Central Staff Organisation and has a Vice Chief of the Defence Staff (VCDS) who ranks as number four in the services hierarchy, following the three single service commanders. The November 1996 announcement that General Sir Charles Gutherie is to replace Field Marshal Sir Peter Inge in the post of CDS probably means that the previous policy of rotating the post of CDS between the heads of the three armed services has ceased.

General Sir Charles Guthrie GCB LVO OBE ADC Chief of The Defence Staff (with effect from 1 May 1997)

General Sir Charles Guthrie was born on 17 November 1938. He went to The Royal Military Academy Sandhurst in 1957 and was commissioned into the Welsh Guards in 1959. He served with his Regiment as a young officer in the United Kingdom, Germany and Aden. In 1966 he became a Troop Commander with 22nd Special Air Service Regiment and served in Aden, the Persian Gulf, Malaysia and East Africa. In 1968 as a Squadron Commander, still serving with 22nd Special Air Service Regiment he served in the Persian Gulf and the United Kingdom.

He returned to 1st Battalion Welsh Guards in Munster in 1970 to command a mechanised infantry company prior to attending the Staff College at Camberley in 1972. His first appointment after attending the Staff College was Military Assistant to the Chief of the General Staff (Field Marshal Lord Carver and General Sir Peter Hunt). After a year as Second in Command of 1st Battalion Welsh Guards in London and Cyprus in 1976 he assumed the appointment of Brigade Major, Household Division. In 1977 he commanded 1st Battalion Welsh Guards in Berlin and Northern Ireland.

General Guthrie became Colonel General Staff, Ministry of Defence in 1980 (Col GS MO2) responsible for military operations and planning worldwide, less Germany and Northern Ireland. In the same year he was Commander British Forces New Hebrides (Vanuatu). In 1981 he was appointed Commander of the 4th Armoured Brigade in Munster, following which he was Chief of Staff, Headquarters 1st (British) Corps in Bielefeld.

He was appointed General Officer Commanding the 2nd Infantry Division and North East District in 1985. He was appointed Colonel Commandant of the Intelligence Corps in 1986. He became Assistant Chief of the General Staff in November 1987 and assumed command of the 1st (British) Corps in October 1989. In January 1992 he became Commander Northern Army Group and Commander in Chief British Army of the Rhine. Northern Army Group was disbanded in June 1993. He was appointed ADC Gen on 13 July 1993 and GCB in The Queen's Birthday Honours List in 1994. On 15 March 1994 he was appointed Chief of the General Staff and on the 1st May 1997 he was appointed Chief of the Defence Staff.

Chain of Command

The Chief of the Defence Staff (CDS) commands and coordinates the activities of the three services through the following chain of command:

General Sir Charles Guthrie - Chief of The Defence Staff

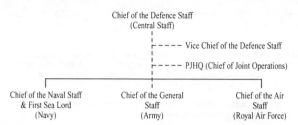

Chief of the Defence Staff
(Central Staff)

- - - - Vice Chief of the Defence Staff

- - - - PJHQ (Chief of Joint Operations)

| Chief of the Naval Staff
& First Sea Lord
(Navy) | Chief of the General
Staff
(Army) | Chief of the Air
Staff
(Royal Air Force) |

The three single service commanders exercise command of their services through their respective headquarters. However, the complex interservice nature of the majority of modern military operations, where military, air and naval support must be coordinated has led to the recent plans for a permanent tri-service Joint Headquarters.

Permanent Joint Headquarters (PJHQ)

The UK MoD established a permanent Joint Headquarters at Northwood in Middlesex for joint military operations on 1 April 1996. This new headquarters brings together on a permanent basis intelligence, planning, operational and logistics staffs. It contains elements of a rapidly deployable in-theatre Joint Force Headquarters that will command rapid deployment front line forces.

In early 1996 MOD officials described the role of PJHQ as "Working proactively to anticipate crises and monitoring developments in areas of interest to the UK. The establishment of PJHQ will set in place a proper, clear and unambiguous connection between policy and the strategic direction and conduct of operations. Because it will exist on a permanent basis rather than being established for a particular operation, as under current arrangements, the permanent Joint HQ will be involved from the very start of planning for a possible operation. It will then take responsibility for the subsequent execution of those plans if necessary."

PJHQ, commanded by the Chief of Joint Operations (CJO), Lieutenant General CBQ Wallace, OBE occupies existing accommodation above and below ground and brings together at Northwood some 330 civilian, specialist and tri-service military staff from across the MoD. There are approximately 90 x Royal Navy, 100 Army, 100 RAF and 40 civilian staff.

PJHQ is responsible for planning all UK led joint, potentially joint, combined and multinational operations and will work in close partnership with MoD Head Office in the planning of operations and policy formulation, thus ensuring PJHQ is well placed to implement policy. Having planned the operation, and contributed advice to Ministers, PJHQ will then conduct such operations.

When another nation is in the lead, PJHQ will exercise operational command of UK forces deployed on the operation.

Being a permanent joint Headquarters, PJHQ will provide continuity of experience from the planning phase to the execution of the operation, and on to post operation evaluation and learning of lessons.

From 1 Aug 1996 PJHQ assumed responsibility for current operations in the Middle East and the Former Yugoslavia.

Non-core functions, such as the day to day management of the Overseas Commands in Cyprus, Falkland Islands, Gibraltar and Hong Kong, are also being delegated by MoD Head Office to the PJHQ. This will allow MoD Head Office to concentrate in particular on policy formulation and strategic direction. The start up cost of PJHQ is estimated to be approximately £6.7 million and the annual running costs of the Headquarters is estimated to be some £16 million.

The Headquarters structure follows the normal Divisional organisation, but staff will operate within multi-disciplinary groups which draw from across the HQ.

PJHQ Headquarters Structure

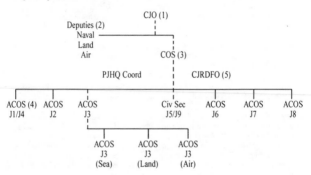

Notes:
(1) CJO Chief of Joint Operations; (2) Deputies to the single Service Commanders in Chief. They provide high level single Service advice to CJO and direct links with single Service commands; (3) COS Chief of Staff; (4) ACOS Assistant Chief of Staff; (5) CJRDFO Chief of the Joint Rapid Deployment Force Operations.

J1 Personnel and Admin.	J6 Communication and Information Systems
J2 Intelligence	J7 Doctrine and Training
J3 Operations	J8 Plans
J4 Logistics	J9 Finance
J5 Policy	

Joint Rapid Deployment Force (JRDF)

Established in August 1996, the JRDF provides a force for rapid deployment operations using a core operational group of the Army's 5th Airborne Brigade and the Royal Navy's 3rd Commando Brigade, supported by a wide range of air force and maritime assets. The force uses what the MoD has described as a 'golf-bag' approach with a wide range of units available for specific operations. For example, if the operational situation demands assets such as heavy armour, long range artillery and attack helicopters, these assets can easily be assigned to the force. This approach means that the RJDF can be tailored for specific operations ranging from support for a humanitarian crisis to operations including high intensity operations.

The 'reach' of the JRDF will be enhanced by the Royal Navy's new amphibious vessels HMS Albion and HMS Bulwark, due to enter service in 2001. Both of these ships will be able to carry 650 troops plus a range of armoured vehicles including main battle tanks. A flight deck will allow ship to shore helicopter operations. The cost of each ship is believed to be in the region of £220 million.

Responsibility for providing units to the JRDF remains with the single service commands who ensure that units assigned are at extremely high state of readiness.

JRDF units remain committed to NATO and from April 1997 the JRDF assigned battalion group will provide the UK commitment to the Allied Command Europe Mobile Force (Land).

The force commander is the CJRDFO (Chief of the Joint Rapid Deployment Force) who is responsible to the Chief of Joint Operations (CJO) at PJHQ. CJRDFO is supported by the Joint Force Operations Staff at PJHQ who would provide the staff element of the RJDF should the force be deployed on operations.

The United Kingdom Defence Budget

> *"You need three things to win a war,*
> *Money, money and more money."*

> Trivulzio (1441-1518)

Current UK Government plans are to spend the following amounts on defence (in real terms) during the next three years:-

> 1997-98 - £21.11 billion.
> 1998-99 - £20.86 billion.
> 1999-00 - £20.96 billion.

Overall Defence Expenditure has fallen by 8.5% in real terms since 1994 and by 1998-1999 defence exenditure will account for 2.7% of GDP (Gross Domestic Product) slightly above the European average of 2.3%. In 1986 the UK defence budget accounted for 5.1% of GDP.

The total Central Government Expenditure plans for the FY 1997-98 Financial Year are budgeted at £314,700 billion and for comparison purposes the Government's major expenditure programmes inside this total are as follows:

Social Security	£93.84 billion
Health	£34.69 billion
Local Authorities (Government Financed)	£31.38 billion
Scotland, Wales & Northern Ireland	£29.45 billion
Debt Interest	£24.80 billion

Defence	£21.11 billion
Education and Employment	£13.95 billion
Local Authorities (Self Financed)	£13.70 billion
Environment (Including housing)	£7.60 billion
Home Office (Including Law & Order)	£6.78 billion
Transport	£5.19 billion
Agriculture (including BSE costs)	£3.61 billion
Trade and Industry	£3.05 billion
Overseas Development	£2.22 billion

The breakdown of the 1996-97 Defence Budget figure of £21.42 billion can be shown in percentage terms for all three services as follows:

Equipment Purchases	-	39.4%
Service Personnel	-	28.9% (pay & allowances)
Civilian Personnel	-	10.9%
Works, Buildings & Land	-	8.7%
Miscellaneous Stores etc	-	12.1%

The equipment expenditure figure can be broken down further, to reveal that during the 1996-97 Financial Year a total of £5.8 billion will be spent, with money going to the services as follows:

Sea Systems	-	£1.999 billion
Land/Army Systems	-	£1.594 billion
Air Systems	-	£3.444 billion
General Support	-	£2.015 billion *
Total	-	£9.052 billion

Note: In general Sea, Land and Air Systems relate to Naval, Army and Air Force expenditure.
* General Support includes £594 million for research and £194 million for development.

The same budget (looked at from a slightly different angle) shows the defence equipment programme as follows:

Repair and spares	£2,587 million	28.6%
General Support	£2,015 million	22.3%
Aircraft Systems	£1,580 million	17.5%
Land Systems	£766 million	8.5%
Weapons and Electronic Systems	£619 million	6.8%
Underwater Systems	£403 million	4.5%
Command Information Systems	£397 million	4.4%
Surface Ships	£376 million	4.1%
Strategic Systems	£309 million	3.3%
Total	£9,052 million	100.0%

Land Equipment Procurement

Some of the more interesting Army equipment expenditure figures (production and repair estimates) for the 1996-97 Financial Year are among the following:

Guns, Small Arms and NBC Defence Stores	- £22	million
Ammunition, Mines and Explosives	- £134	million
Fighting Vehicles	- £272	million
Load Carrying Vehicles	- £145	million
Engineering Equipment	- £61	million
Guided Weapons	- £141	million
Communications	- £175	million
Surveillance Equipment	- £71	million
Maintenance	- £376	million

Army Expenditure (Top Level Budget Holders TLB)

During 1996-97 Army expenditure figures for the top level budget holders are among the following:

UK Land Forces

Scotland	-	£98.2	million
London District	-	£164.1	million
UK Support Commang (Germany)	-	£374.3	million
1st (UK) Armoured Division	-	£717.1	million
2nd Division	-	£350.0	million
3rd (UK) Division	-	£273.7	million
4th (UK) Division	-	£499.7	million
5th Division	-	£182.3	million
Reserves & Cadets	-	£92.9	million
GOC Northern Ireland	-	£493.9	million
Total	-	£2,930.7	million

Army Personnel - Adjutant General (TLB)

Manning, Recruitment & Training	-	£169.4	million
Service Childrens Education	-	£48.1	million
Personnel Management	-	£113.7	million
Army Individual Training	-	£454.8	million
Chief of Staff	-	£53.8	million
Total	-	£1,054.8	million

Army Logistics - Quartermaster General (TLB)

Equipment Support	-	£474.9	million
Logistic Support	-	£398.2	million
Logistic Policy & Services	-	£54.1	million
Information Systems*	-	£51.0	million
Total	-	£976.1	million

* Includes information technology support, engineer services and logistic planning.

The high unit costs of individual items of equipment illustrate the problems faced by defence planners when working out their annual budgets. At 1996 prices the following items cost:

Kinetic Energy Round for Challenger	£1,750 each
Individual Weapon (IW)	£550 each
5.56mm round for IW	£0.90
One Rapier Missile	£40,000
One Challenger Tank	£2.5 million (approx)
Tornado Air Defence Fighter	£23 million
PRC 351 VHF Radio	£6,000 each
Combat High Boot	£50 per pair
Harrier GR5	£14.2 million
Lynx Helicopter	£6.25 million
Starstreak Missile	£100,000 each
Trigat (MR) Missile	£30,000 each (estimate).
Attack Helicopter	£25 million (region)

Defence Budgets - NATO Comparison

For ease of conversions from national currencies, amounts are shown in US$.

The nations of the North Atlantic Treaty Organisation (NATO), of which the United Kingdom is a member state, spent some US$437.2 billion on defence during 1996,

NATO Defence Budget Analysis

NATO Defence Expenditure 1996	-	US$437.2 billion
NATO Defence Expenditure 1996 (less USA)	-	US$181.9 billion
NATO (European Nations) Defence Expenditure 1996	-	US$173.9 billion

The next table shows the defence budget for each NATO nation during 1996.

USA	US$ 255.3	billion
France	US$ 38.4	billion
UK	US$ 32.4	billion
Germany	US$ 31.9	billion
Italy	US$ 19.9	billion
Netherlands	US$ 8.0	billion
Canada	US$ 7.7	billion
Spain	US$ 6.9	billion
Turkey	US$ 6.6	billion
Norway	US$ 3.7	billion
Greece	US$ 3.4	billion
Belgium	US$ 3.2	billion
Denmark	US$ 3.1	billion
Portugal	US$ 1.7	billion
Luxembourg	US$ 121	million

Note: Iceland has no military expenditure although it remains a member of NATO.

An interesting comparison is made by the total national defence budget divided by the total number of full time personnel in all three services. Figures for the top six world defence spending nations are as follows:-

Ranking	Nation	1996 Defence Budget	Total Service Personnel	Cost Per Serviceman
1	USA	US$55.37 bn	1,483, 000	US$172,151
2	Russia	US$48.0 bn	1,270,000	US$37,795
3	Japan	US$45.1 bn	235,500	US$191,507
4	France	US$38.4 bn	398,900	US$92,624
5	UK	US$32.4 bn	222,300	US$145,748
6	Germany	US$31.9 bn	358,400	US$89,006

Note: We show Russia as the second nation in this table but estimates of Russian defence expenditure show wide variations. In this table we have used the IISS (International Institute of Strategic Studies) estimate of the 1996 Russian defence budget. However the true figure may be less than the US$48 billion shown. Some analysts believe that the exact figure may be in the region of about US$30 billion.

British Army Statistics

Strength of The Regular Army (1 May 1996)

Armour	11 Regiments (1)
Royal Artillery	16 Regiments (2)
Royal Engineers	10 Regiments
Infantry	41 Battalions (3)
Special Air Service	1 Regiment
Army Air Corps	5 Regiments (5)
Signals	12 Regiments (4)
Equipment Support	5 Battalions
Logistics	26 Regiments (6)
Medical	12 Hospitals/Field Ambulances

Notes: (1) Includes 1 x Training Regiment. (2) Includes 1 x Training Regiment. (3) Excludes the 6 x Battalions that comprise the Home Service Element of the Royal Irish Regiment and 1 x Battalion of the Gibraltar Regiment. (5) Includes 1 x Training Regiment. (6) Includes 3 x Combat Service Support Battalions that have a mix of REME,RAMC and RLC personnel). In general these Battalions/Regiments are commanded by Lt Colonels and have a strength of between 500 and 800 personnel.

Strength of the Territorial Army (1 May 1996)

Armour	5 Regiments (1)
Royal Artillery	6 Regiments (2)
Royal Engineers	9 Regiments
Infantry	36 Battalions
Special Air Service	2 Regiments

Signals	11 Regiments	
Equipment Support	5 Battalions	
Logistics	11 Regiments	
Medical	18 Hospitals/Field Ambulances	

Notes: (1) Includes 4 x Regional National Defence Reconnaissance Regiments and 1 x Armoured Reconnaissance Regiment. (2) Includes Honourable Artillery Company (HAC).

Deployment of The Regular Army (As at 1 May 1996)

	Officers	Soldiers
Land Command		
1st (UK) Armoured Division	1,200	15,500
2nd Division	700	8,100
3rd (UK) Division	700	7,700
4th Division	1,100	13,300
5th Division	400	4,200
Scotland	200	1,500
London District	400	3,900
UK Support Command (Germany)	700	3,400
Miscellaneous & Administration	1,000	2,500
	6,500	**60,300**
Northern Ireland	800	9,700
Adjutant General (Personnel & Training Command)		
Manning & Training	-	200
Personnel Management	200	100
Army Individual Training	1,200	5,200
Army Personnel in Training	2,100	10,800
Chief of Staff	600	1,300
	4,100	**17,600**
Quartermaster General		
Equipment Support	200	300
Logistic Support	300	1,000
Logistic Policy & Services	100	300
	600	**1,600**

Overseas Garrisons		
	Army	
Falkland Islands	800 (approx)	1,700
Gibraltar	63	695
Hong Kong	454	1,770
Other Far East	194	565
Brunei	820	830
Cyprus	2,807	4,315
Other Near East & Gulf	216	616
Other Locations	3,053	8,390

Note: The figures in brackets relate to tri-service garrisons. Figures for other locations include personnel on short tours and detached from HQ Land. These figures do not include UK Army personnel in the Former Yugoslavia.

Manning Figures (Including personnel under training)

Regular Army (As at 1 April 1996)

	1996	1990
Trained Officers	12,800	16,200
Trained Soldiers	87,200	121,000
Untrained Officers	1,000	1,200
Untrained Soldiers	8,300	14,400
	109,400	152,800

Note: 1990 Figures are given for comparison purposes.

Regular Army Reserves (As at 1 April 1996)

	1996	1990
Regular Reserves	196,000	133,100
Territorial Army	58,700	63,300

Recruitment - Regular Army (During Financial Year 1995/96)

	(1995-96)	(1980/81)
Officers	891	1,489
Soldiers	12,020	27,382
Total	12,991	28,871

Note: 1980/81 figures are given for comparison.

Army Recruitment Targets and Achievement (Soldiers)

Year	Target	Achievement
1990-91	15,230	15,305
1991-92	15,220	15,290
1992-93	12,300	10,000
1993-94	9,200	8,700
1994-95	11,200	9,289
1995-96	-	12,020

Army Recruitment Targets and Achievement (Officers)

Year	Target	Achievement
1990-91	800	825
1991-92	800	810
1992-93	611	537
1993-94	600	587
1994-95	730	609
1995-96	-	891

Outflow - Regular Army (During Financial Year 1995/96)

	(1995-96)	(1990/91)	(1980/81)
Officers	1,289	1,860	1,497
Soldiers	14,154	20,964	20,422
Total	15,443	22,824	21,919

Army Cadet Force

	(1 Apr 1994)	(1 Apr 1980)
Total Cadets	65,400	74,600

Total expenditure on the Cadet Forces during FY 19956 was £22.55 million for the Army Cadet Force (ACF) and £3.74 million for the Combined Cadet Force (CCF) Army Detachment.

UK Army Establishment Figures 1 May 1996 (Trained Personnel)

	Soldiers	Officers
Household Cavalry/Royal Armoured Corps	5, 121	884
Royal Artillery	7,652	1,132
Royal Engineers	7,810	1,147
Royal Signals	8,321	999
Infantry	24,913	2,915
Army Air Corps	1,317	350
Royal Logistic Corps	14,807	1,821
Royal Army Medical Corps	1,878	704
Royal Electrical and Mechanical Engineers	9,476	895
Adjutant General's Corps	5,990	1,116
Royal Army Veterinary Corps	159	24
Small Arms School Corps	100	27
Royal Army Dental Corps	243	160
Intelligence Corps	1,055	273
Army Physical Training Corps	300	39
Queen Alexandra's Royal Army Nursing Corps	556	395
RAChD	-	144
Long Service List	496	-
Army Musicians	1,136	35
Gurkhas	4,325	155
	95,655	**12,845**

Animals on Strength (As at 1 Nov 1996)

Horses	483
Dogs	1,800
Goats	2 (Regimental Mascots)
Black Buck	1 (Regimental Mascot)
Ram	1 (Regimental Mascot)
Shetland Pony	2 (Regimental Mascots)
Wolf Hound	1 (Regimental Mascot)
Drum Horse	1 (Regimental Mascot)
Ferret	1 (Regimental Mascot)*

Note: The ferret held by 1st Battalion the Prince of Wale's Own Regiment of Yorkshire is not a charge to public funds.

100 Years Ago - Strength of the British Army

Household Cavalry	1,316
Cavalry of the Line	18,388
Horse Artillery	3,781
Field Artillery	14,308
Mountain Artillery	1,293
Garrison Artillery	17,312
Royal Engineers	7,424
Foot Guards	6,032
Infantry of the Line	135,175
Colonial Corps	5,070
Army Service Corps	3,523
Ordnance Staff	857
Armourers	318
Medical Services	2,482
	217,279

CHAPTER 2 - ARMY ORGANISATIONS

"The typical staff officer is the man well past middle life, spare, unwrinkled, intelligent, cold, passive, noncommittal; with eyes like a codfish, polite in contact but at the same time unresponsive, cool and calm and as damnably composed as a concrete post or a plaster of Paris cast; a human petrification with a heart of feldspar and without charm or the friendly germ; minus bowels, passion, or a sense humour. Happily they never reproduce and all of them finally go to hell."

Anon

The routine management of the Army is the responsibility of The Army Board the composition of which is shown in the next diagram.

The Army Board
The Secretary of State for Defence
Minister of State (Armed Forces)
Minister of State (Defence Procurement)
Parliamentary UnderSecretary of State for the Armed Forces
Chief of the General Staff
Second Permanent Under Secretary of State
Adjutant General
Quartermaster General
Master General of the Ordnance
Commander in Chief (Land Command)
Commander UK Support Command (Germany)
Assistant Chief of the General Staff

Decisions made by the Army Board are acted upon by the military staff at the various headquarters world-wide. The Chief of the General Staff is the officer responsible for the Army's contribution to the national defence effort and he maintains control through the commander and the staff branches of each of these headquarters. Each military headquarters is organised along exactly the same lines with identical branches at each level in the chain of command.

General Sir Roger Wheeler KCB CBE
Chief of the General Staff (CGS)

General Sir Roger Wheeler, a member of an established military family, was commissioned direct from Oxford University into his father's regiment, The Royal Ulster Rifles in 1964, joining the 1st Battalion in Borneo.

After some years of regimental service he attended the Command and Staff College, Queenscliffe, Australia, and in 1974 was appointed Brigade Major at 19 Airportable Brigade in Colchester. During this tour the Brigade was deployed to Cyprus for the 1974 emergency.

Two years later he rejoined his battalion, now the 2nd Battalion The Royal Irish Rangers, in West Germany, before leaving in 1977 to command the senior NCOs division of the School of Infantry, Brecon. Later that year he joined Field Marshal Lord Carver, who had been appointed as the Resident Military Commissioner (designate), in Rhodesia as a member of his staff.

In 1978, promoted to Lieutenant Colonel, he took up a post with the Chief of the Defence Staff, after which he assumed command of the 2nd Battalion Royal Irish Rangers in 1979 in Tidworth. During this period of command the Battalion served in Belize, as well as carrying out exercises in Canada and Gibraltar, before moving to Berlin.

In May 1983, on promotion to Colonel, he was posted to HQ UKLF, but left almost immediately for the Falklands as Chief of Staff for 6 months, before returning to HQ UKLF to reassume his original appointment.

In December 1984, now promoted to Brigadier, he took command of 11th Armoured Brigade in Minden, West Germany after which he held the appointment of Director Army Plans in MoD from 1987 to 1989.

He was promoted to Major General in August 1989 assuming command of the 1st Armoured Division in BAOR until November 1990 when he assumed the appointment of Assistant Chief of the General Staff until December 1993.

General Wheeler was appointed GOC Northern Ireland in January 1993, a post he held for 3 years, until becoming Commander in Chief Land Command in March 1996, at the same time being appointed Joint Commander for the British forces deployed in Bosnia with IFOR. In May 1997 he was appointed Chief of the General Staff.

Staff Branches

The Staff Branches that you would expect to find at every military headquarters from the Ministry of Defence (MoD) down to Brigade level are as follows:

Commander	-	Usually a general who commands the formation.
Chief of Staff	-	The officer who runs the headquarters on a day-to-day basis and who often acts as a second-in-command.
G1 Branch	-	Responsible for personnel matters including manning, discipline and personal services.
G2 Branch	-	Responsible for intelligence and security.
G3 Branch	-	Responsible for operations including staff duties, exercise planning, training, operational requirements, combat development & tactical doctrine.
G4 Branch	-	Logistics and quartering.
G5 Branch	-	Civil and military co-operation

The Army is controlled from the MoD via two subsidiary headquarters and a number of smaller headquarters world-wide. The Joint Headquarters (JHQ) at Northwood in Middlesex (described in Chapter 1) has an important input into this chain of command and it is almost certain that any operation with which the Army is involved will be under the overall command of PJHQ. The following diagram illustrates this chain of command.

General Sir Roger Wheeler - Chief of The General Staff

HQ Land Command

Following the MoD's Front Line First study, plans were drawn up to reorganise HQ United Kingdom Land Forces (HQ UKLF) in a new formation designated HQ Land Command that became operational on 1 April 1995. HQ Land Command is located at Erskine Barracks, Wilton near Salisbury and controls about 75% of the troops in the British Isles and almost 100% of its fighting capability.

Land Command's role is to deliver and sustain the Army's operational capability, whenever required throughout the world, and the Command comprises all oprational troops in Great Britain, Germany, Nepal and Brunei, together with the Army Training Teams in Canada, Belize and Kenya. Land Command has almost 70,000 trained Army personnel - the largest single Top Level Budget in Defence, with a budget of just under £3 Billion. It contains all the Army's fighting equipment, including attack helicopters, Challenger 2 tanks, Warrior Infantry Fighting Vehicles, AS90 (the new artillery gun) and the Multi-Launched Rocket System (MLRS).

Land Command is one of the three central commands in the British Army, the other two being the Adjutant General (with responsibility for administration, personnel and training) and the Quartermaster General (responsible for supply and logistics). The Command is responsible for providing all the Army's fighting troops throughout the World. These are organised into eight formations and are commanded by Major Generals.

Chain of Command

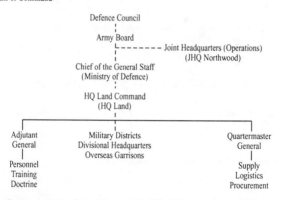

Note: Garrisons in Northern Ireland, Cyprus and the Falkland Islands are commanded from the MoD via JHQ.

Ready Divisions

There are two "Ready" Divisions: the 1st (UK) Armoured Division, based in Germany, and the 3rd (UK) Division in the United Kingdom. Both of these divisions are earmarked to form part of the Allied

Command Europe Rapid Reaction Corps (ARRC), NATO's premier strategic formation; but they also have the flexibility to be employed on rapid reaction tasks or in support of other Defence Roles.

In addition to their operational roles, they also command the Army units in specified geographic areas: in the case of the 1st Division, this area is made up of the garrisons in Germany where the Division's units are based; and in the case of the 3rd Division, the South West of England.

Regenerative Divisions

Three Regenerative Divisions, based on old Districts in the United Kingdom. These are the 2nd Division (replacing Eastern District) with its Headquarters at York, the 4th Division with its Headquarters at Aldershot, and the 5th Division (replacing the old Wales and Western District) with its Headquarters at Shrewsbury. These Regenerative Divisions are responsible for all Army units within their boundaries, and could provide the core for three new divisions, should the Army be required to expand to meet a major international threat.

Districts

Three Districts remain: Scotland, London, and the United Kingdom Support Command (Germany). Scotland and London are responsible for all Army units within their boundaries; the United Kingdom Support Command (Germany) with its Headquarters at Rheindahlen has similar responsibilities, but also provides essential support functions for the 1st Division and the Headquarters of the ARRC.

These eight divisions or district areas are further sub-divided into brigades and garrisons, which also have a varying mix of operational and infrastructure support responsibilities. As a result of the Defence Costs Studies, some brigade headquarters, which previously had purely operational functions, have been amalgamated with garrison headquarters to achieve savings and greater efficiency.

Embedded into this structure are all the other force elements which represent Land Command's operational capability. They include:

24 Airmobile Brigade, based in Colchester and under the command of the 4th Division for operations is part of the MultiNational Division (Centre), an airmobile Division with its headquarters in Rheindahlen.

The United Kingdom element of the ACE Mobile Force (Land), with its Headquarters and logistic elements at Bulford and an infantry battalion at Dover.

Three signal Brigades (one of which is in Germany).

Two Combat Service Support Groups (one of which is in Germany).

Various additional units which are earmarked for the ACE Rapid Reaction Corps or for National Defence tasks.

The overseas detachments in Canada, Belize, Brunei and Nepal are commanded directly from Headquarters Land Command at Wilton. The Review of the Army Command Structure recommended that the Army should be organised into three central commands and that doctrine and training should be the responsibility of the Adjutant General rather than the Commander-in-Chief. Therefore Headquarters Doctrine and Training at Upavon, Wiltshire, does not form part of Land Command (although it was part of United Kingdom Land Forces until 1993).

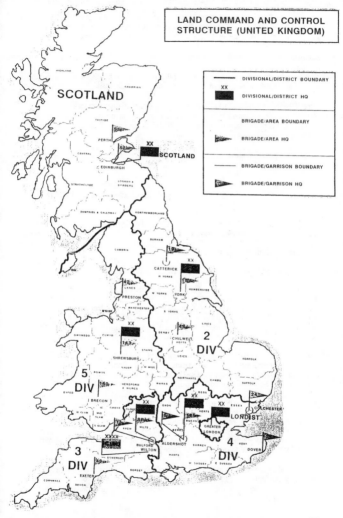

LAND COMMAND AND CONTROL
STRUCTURE (UNITED KINGDOM)

Although Land Command is not responsible for running operations in Northern Ireland, Cyprus and the Falkland Islands (a responsibility of PJHQ), it will provide the operational troops for these areas. Some 12,000 troops are involved in Northern Ireland at present, either deployed in the Province or training for deployment; and a further 5,000 are deployed to Cyprus and the Falklands.

National operations and operations in support of the United Nations/NATO, the most significant of which are 10,000 troops deployed in the Former Yugoslavia (late 1996).

Some 500 troops are involved at any one time in MoD-sponsored equipment trials, demonstrations and exhibitions. Public Duties in London taking up two/ three battalions at any one time. All troops not otherwise operationally committed are also available to provide Military Aid to the Civil Authorities in the United Kingdom.

Headquarters Land Command has assumed a number of new responsibilities, some of which have been delegated from MoD as part of recent reviews. These include:

The Commitments Plot - Control of the Operational Tour Plot, the Arms Plot (the rotation of Armoured, Artillery and Infantry units between stations), the Formation Training Plot, and the provision of assistance to trials and studies.

Collective Training - Including responsibility for armoured battlegroup training at the British Army Training Unit at Suffield in Canada.

Land Command Divisional/District Summaries

1 (UK) Armoured Division & British Forces Germany (BFG)

The 1st Armoured Division was formed in 1940 adopting the charging rhino (the most heavily armoured animal) as its insignia in 1942 prior to El Alamein. Since the Second World War the Division has been retitled three times and became the 1st (United Kingdom) Armoured Division in 1993, having successfully fought in the Gulf War of 1991. The Division has its headquarters at Herford in Germany and commands three Armoured Brigades situated throughout North West Germany and is the major component of British Forces Germany.

British Forces Germany (BFG) is the composite name given to the British Army, Royal Air Force and supporting civil elements stationed in Germany. The terms British Army of the Rhine (BAOR) and Royal Air Force Germany (RAFG), until recently were the traditional names used to describe the two Service elements of the British Forces stationed in Germany.

For many years following WWII, and as a result of the confrontation between NATO and the former Warsaw Treaty Organisation, the UK Government had stationed four Army divisions and a considerable part of its Air Force at five airbases in the Federal Republic of Germany. On the whole this level of commitment was maintained until 1992 and although these forces appeared to be solely national, they were in fact closely integrated with the NATO Northern Army Group (NORTHAG) and the 2nd Allied Tactical Air Force (2 ATAF).

As a result of political changes in Europe and the UK Government's Options for Change programme, the British Army's presence in Germany has been reduced to three armoured brigades and a divisional headquarters. The RAF presence has been concentrated on two airbases (to be reduced to 1 in 1999).

Composition of 1(UK) Armoured Division

1 (UK) Armoured Division has its headquarters at Herford in Germany (about 50kms from Hanover) and the three Armoured Brigades under command are located at Osnabruck, Bergen-Hohne and Paderborn.

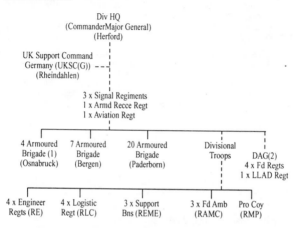

Note: (1) Current plans appear to be for all three armoured brigades to have an identical organisation. (2) DAG (Divisional Artillery Group) This DAG could be reinforced by Rapier Air Defence and MLRS units from the UK as necessary. Personnel total in Germany is 20,800; 16,700 in 1 (UK) Armoured Division and 4,100 in UKSC(G).

This Division could provide the Headquarters (HQs) for 12 Battlegroups.

Force Levels in 1 (UK) Armoured Division (1 April 1996)

Army Personnel	16,700
Challenger MBT	250
Tracked Vehicles	1,350
Army Helicopters	35
Artillery Guns	52
MLRS	0
AVLB	21

It is probable that in the event of hostilities considerable numbers of officers and soldiers from the Territorial Army (TA) would be used to reinforce this division. These reinforcements would consist of individuals, drafts of specialists, or by properly formed TA units varying in size from Mobile Bath Units of 20 men, to Major Units over 500 strong. For example the UK MoD recently announced that eight TA infantry battalions had a role that entailed possible support for the ARRC.

UKSC(G) - The United Kingdom Support Command (Germany) has responsibility for British Army Troops on the Continent of Europe that are not part of 1st (United Kingdom) Armoured Division. Its headquarters replaces that of the British Army of the Rhine, whose sign it has adopted. The new headquarters is located at Rheindahlen.

2nd Division

The 2nd Division has responsibility for the whole of Eastern England excluding Essex. Though the Division was first formed in 1809 to fight in the Peninsular War, the crossed keys sign was not adopted until 1940 when the division was reconstituted in England following the withdrawal from Dunkirk. Its most famous engagement was during the Burma Campaign in 1944 when, at the battle for Kohima, the tide against the Japanese Army finally turned. The Divisional Headquarters is in York.

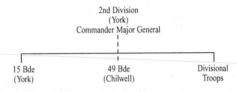

```
                          2nd Division
                            (York)
                   Commander Major General
                              |
      ┌───────────────────────┼───────────────────────┐
   15 Bde                  49 Bde                  Divisional
   (York)                 (Chilwell)                 Troops
```

Force Levels in 2nd Division (1 April 1996)

Army Personnel	8,800
Challenger MBT	50
Tracked Vehicles	499
Army Helicopters	32
Artillery Guns	51
MLRS	3
AVLB	0

3 (UK) Division

The 3rd (United Kingdom) Division is the only operational (Ready) Division in the UK. The Division has a mix of capabilities encompassing armoured, airborne and wheeled elements in its two mechanised brigades and one airborne brigade. The Division which was first formed during the Napoleonic Wars now also has responsibility for South-West England. The Iron-Triangle insignia was chosen for it in the early part of World War II by its commander the then, Major General B L Montgomery.

Following plans for the reorganisation of NATO Forces on the Central Front during 1992, the HQ of the 3rd (UK) Armoured Division moved from is old location at Soest in Germany to Bulford in Wiltshire, where it became 3(UK) Division and part of the NATO ARRC (Allied Rapid Reaction Corps). In the event of hostilities it will move to the ARRC area of operations on the European mainland or worldwide as necessary.

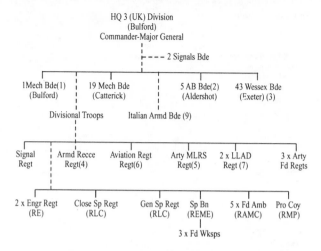

HQ 3 (UK) Division
(Bulford)
Commander-Major General

---- 2 Signals Bde

| 1 Mech Bde(1) | 19 Mech Bde | 5 AB Bde(2) | 43 Wessex Bde |
| (Bulford) | (Catterick) | (Aldershot) | (Exeter) (3) |

Divisional Troops   Italian Armd Bde (9)

| Signal Regt | Armd Recce Regt(4) | Aviation Regt Regt(6) | Arty MLRS Regt(5) | 2 x LLAD Regt (7) | 3 x Arty Fd Regts |

| 2 x Engr Regt (RE) | Close Sp Regt (RLC) | Gen Sp Regt (RLC) | Sp Bn (REME) | 5 x Fd Amb (RAMC) | Pro Coy (RMP) |

3 x Fd Wksps

Note: (1) 1 Mechanised Brigade; (2) 5 Airborne Brigade; (3) 43 Bde is a mainly TA formation with a mobilisation role in support of 3(UK) Div. (4) Armoured Reconnaissance Regiment; (5) Artillery Regiment with Multi Launch Rocket System; (6) Army Air Corps Regiment with Lynx & Gazelle; (7) Air Defence Regiments with Rapier and Javelin/Starstreak missiles;(8) The composition of this division with a lightly armed parachute brigade plus a Marine Commando Brigade allows the UK MoD to retain a balanced force for out of NATO area operations should that become necessary (9) Under Allied Rapid Reaction Corps framework agreements this division could be reinforced by an Italian Armoured Brigade (Ariete). 3 Commando Brigade a Royal Naval formation is available to support 3(UK) Div if necessary. Details of the organisation of 3 Cdo Bde are given in the Miscellaneous Chapter. 3 Cdo Bde is not under the command of 3 Div.

Force Levels in 3 (UK) Division (1 April 1996)

Army Personel	8400
Challenger MBT	93
Tracked Vehicles	1,280
Army Helicopters	21
Artillery Guns	154
MLRS	24
AVLB	27

Note: Under the figure for main battle tanks there are a further 235 Chieftain; the majority of which are believed to be in store awaiting disposal.

4th Division

The 4th Division has military responsibility for South East England, including Bedfordshire, Essex and Hertfordshire and its Headqarters is in Aldershot. It was previously based in Germany until 1992 as an armoured division. The division now has three brigades under command, 2 Brigade based in Shorncliffe, 24 Brigade in Colchester and 145 Brigade in Aldershot. The divisional symbol is the Tiger.

4th Division
(Aldershot)
Commander Major General

┝ ─ ─ ─ Divisional Troops

| 2 Bde | 145 Bde | 24 Airmobile Bde |
| (Shorncliffe) | (Aldershot) | (Colchester) |

Force Levels in 4th Division (1 April 1996)

Army Personnel	13,400
Challenger MBT	26
Tracked Vehicles	1,280
Army Helicopters	21
Artillery Gun	154
MLRS	24
AVLB	27

5th Division

The 5th Division has responsibility for military units and establishments in Wales, the West Midlands and the North West of England and its Headquarters is in Shrewsbury. The Division emblem, inherited from Wales and Western District, depicts the Welsh Dragon, the cross of St Chad (7th Century Bishop of Mercia), and the Red Rose of Lancaster. The Fifth Division fought at Waterloo and played a significant part in the endeavours of the BEF in both World Wars.

5th Division
(Shrewsbury)
Commander Major General

11 (ARRC) Signals Bde ─ ─ ─ ─ ┼ ─ ─ ─ ─ Divisional Troops

| 42 Bde | 143 Bde | 160 Bde |
| (Preston) | (Shrewsbury) | (Brecon) |

Force Levels in 5th Division (1 April 1996)

Army Personnel	4,600
Challenger MBT	0
Tracked Vehicles	123
Army Helicopters	2
Artillery Guns	97
MLRS	1
AVLB	0

Scottish District

The Army in Scotland is commanded from a Headquarters at Craigiehall, Edinburgh which has responsibility for the entire national territory of Scotland including the Western and Northern Islands. The distinguishing flag of Army Headquarters Scotland is a Lion Rampant superimposed on a black and red background.

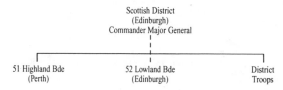

Scottish District
(Edinburgh)
Commander Major General

51 Highland Bde	52 Lowland Bde	District
(Perth)	(Edinburgh)	Troops

Force Levels in Scottish District (1 April 1996)

Army Personnel	1,700
Challenger MBT	0
Tracked Vehicles	3
Army Helicopters	0
Artillery Guns	0
MLRS	0
AVLB	0

London District

Headquarters London District was formed in 1906. It has responsibility for units that are located within the Greater London Area as well as in Windsor. The activity for which the Headquarters and the District is most well known is State Ceremonial and Public Duties in the Capital. The district insignia shows the Sword of St Paul representing the City of London and the Mural Crown representing the County of London. The District has its Headquarters in Horse Guards.

London District
(Horse Guards)
Commander Major General

Public Duties
Battalions

District
Troops

Force Levels in London District (1 April 1996)

Army Personnel	4,300
Challenger MBT	0
Tracked Vehicles	4
Army Helicopters	0
Artillery Guns	26
MLRS	0
AVLB	0

Army Brigades

The Armoured Brigade

The following diagram illustrates the possible composition of an Armoured Brigade in 1(UK) Armd Div on operations.

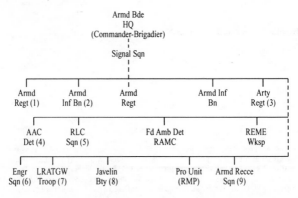

Armd Bde
HQ
(Commander-Brigadier)

Signal Sqn

Armd
Regt (1)

Armd
Inf Bn (2)

Armd
Regt

Armd Inf
Bn

Arty
Regt (3)

AAC
Det (4)

RLC
Sqn (5)

Fd Amb Det
RAMC

REME
Wksp

Engr
Sqn (6)

LRATGW
Troop (7)

Javelin
Bty (8)

Pro Unit
(RMP)

Armd Recce
Sqn (9)

Totals: 76 x Challenger MBT (Possibly)
90 x Warrior AIFV
80 x AFV 432 APC
24 x AS 90 SP Gun
Approx 4,500 men

Notes: (1) Armoured Regiment with approx 38 x Challenger MBT; (2) Armoured Inf Battalion with approx 45 x Warrior (with rifle coys) and approx 40 x FV432; (3) Artillery Regiment with 32 AS90 SP Guns; (4) Army Air Corps Detachment (possibly 9 x Lynx & 4 x Gazelle); (5) Transport Squadron RLC with approximately 60 -70 trucks; (6) Engineer Squadron with 68 vehicles but depending upon the task could involve a complete engineer battalion; (7) Long Range Anti-Tank Guided Weapon Troop (Swingfire) but due to be replaced by Trigat(LR) in the longer term; (8) RA Bty with 36 x Javelin AD missiles and 40 vehicles; (9) Armoured Recce Squadron.

This Brigade could provide the HQs for 4 Battlegroups

Mechanised Brigade Organisation

The following is an example of the 3 (UK) Division Mechanised Brigade organisation.

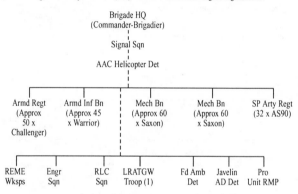

Note: (1) Long Range Anti-Tank Guided Weapons-Currently Striker/Swingfire.

1 Mechanised Brigade Battle Winning Equipment Establishment Table During August 1995.

Equipment	Qty
Chieftain MBT	50
Chieftain ARRV	5
Warrior Command	9
Warrior Section	47
Warrior Repair	8
Warrior Recovery	4
Combat Vehicle Reconnaissance (Tracked)	8
CVR(T) Sultan Command	8
CVR(T) Spartan Multirole transport vehicle	714
CVR(T) Samson REME variant (winch)	4

SAXON Command Vehicles	38
SAXON Section Vehicles	82
SAXON Maintenance	10
Fighting Vehicle (FV) 432 Command	2
FV432 Section Vehicles	28
FV432 Ambulance	10
FV434 REME Repair Vehicle	5
FV436 Communications Vehicle	10
FV439 Radio Relay	2
FV439 Secondary Access Message Centre	2

Note: At the time this table was published 1 RTR (part of 1 Mech Bde) was the last Chieftain Regiment in the army.

5 Airborne Brigade Organisation

The following is an organisational outline of 5 Airborne Brigade (under command 3 (UK) Division) but an important component of the JRDF.

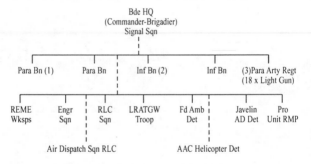

Note: (1) Parachute Battalion ; (2) Infantry Battalion; (3) It is possible that under this new organisation the Para Arty Regt may receive an extra battery bringing the total of Light Guns to 24; The Logistic elements come under the overall command of 5 AB Bde Logistics Bn.

Airmobile Brigade

On 1 April 1988, 24 Infantry Brigade based at Catterick in North Yorkshire, was redesignated 24 Airmobile Brigade with the role of acting as a flexible, high speed anti-tank reserve force. The Brigade moved to Colchester in March 1993, and was enhanced considerably under the "Options for Change" review. Although under command of 4th Division, for operations 24 Airmob Bde now forms part of the Multi National Division - Central (MND(C)) which was formed officially on 1 April 1994. The MND(C) also comprises 31 German Luftlande Brigade, a Belgian Paracommando Brigade and 11 Netherlands Airmobile Brigade, giving the Division the reach, speed and flexibility it will require to be part of the ARRC's most mobile formation.

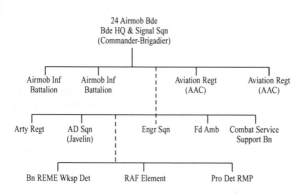

24 Airmob Bde
Bde HQ & Signal Sqn
(Commander-Brigadier)

Airmob Inf Battalion — Airmob Inf Battalion — Aviation Regt (AAC) — Aviation Regt (AAC)

Arty Regt — AD Sqn (Javelin) — Engr Sqn — Fd Amb — Combat Service Support Bn

Bn REME Wksp Det — RAF Element — Pro Det RMP

Note: (1) Support helicopters are provided by the RAF and the Brigade would normally expect to operate with 18 x Chinook and 18 x Puma. An airmobile infantry battalion can be moved by 20 x Chinook equivalents. (2) Each airmobile infantry battalion is equipped with 42 x Milan firing posts - a total of 84 within the Brigade.(3) 3 Regt Army Air Corps and 4 Regt Army Air Corps both of whom are based at RAF Wattisham support 24 Airmob Bde.

The Battlegroup

A division usually consists of 3 brigades. These brigades are further sub-divided into smaller formations known as battlegroups. The battlegroup is the basic building brick of the fighting formations.

A battlegroup is commanded by a Lieutenant Colonel and the infantry battalion or armoured regiment that he commands, provides the command and staff element of the formation. The battlegroup is then structured according to task, with the correct mix of infantry, armour and supporting arms.

The battlegroup organisation is very flexible and the units assigned can be quickly regrouped to cope with a change in the threat. A typical battlegroup fighting a defensive battle on the FEBA (Forward Edge of the Battle Area), and based upon an organisation of one armoured squadron and two mechanised companies, could contain about 600 men, 16 tanks and about 80 armoured personnel carriers.

The number of battlegroups in a division and a brigade could vary according to the task the formation has been given. As a general rule you could expect a division to have as many as 12 battlegroups and a brigade to have up to 4. The following diagram shows a possible organisation for an armoured battlegroup in either 1(UK) Armd Div or 3(UK) Div.

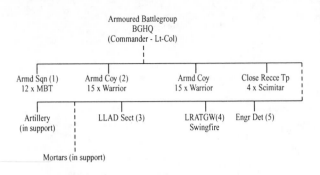

(1) Armoured Squadron
(2) Armoured Company
(3) LLAD-Low Level Air Defence - Javelin
(4) LRATGW - Long Range Anti Tank Guided Weapon Swingfire.
(5) Engineer Detachment

Company Groups

Each battlegroup will operate with smaller organisations called combat teams or company groups. These company groups which are commanded by a Major, will be allocated tanks, armoured personnel carriers and supporting elements depending upon the aim of the formation. Supporting elements such as air defence, antitank missiles, fire support and engineer expertise ensure that the combat team is a balanced all arms grouping, tailored specifically for the task. In general a battlegroup similar to the one in the previous diagram could be expected to form 3 company groups.

Expect a Company Group organisation to resemble the following diagram:

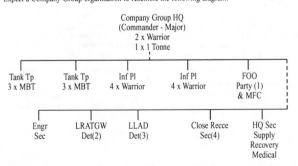

Notes: (1) Forward Observation Officer (FOO usually a Captain) with his party from the Royal Artillery. This FOO will be in direct communication with a battery of eight guns and the Artillery Fire Direction Centre. The MFC is usually a sergeant from an infantry battalion mortar platoon who may have up to six mortar tubes on call. In most Combat Teams both the FOO and MFC will travel in close proximity to the Combat Team Commander; (2) Possibly 2 x Striker with Swingfire; (3) Possibly 2 x Spartan with Javelin; (4) Possibly 2 x Scimitar.

Allied Command Europe Mobile Force Land AMF(L) Contingent

This contingent is the UK's contribution to the Allied Command Europe Mobile Force (AMF) which is tasked with the reinforcement of the flanks of NATO. On mobilisation operations would probably take place in either Norway or Turkey and the UK MoD has recently stated that the UK's contribution to the AMF will be retained. The AMF is a Brigade+ NATO formation with about 6,000 men and 1,500 vehicles.

In 1995 the UK contingent on an AMF(L) exercise in Norway included 1 x Infantry Bn, 1 x Armoured Sqn, 1 Locating Bty, 1 x Artillery Bty, 1 x Signals Sqn, 1 x Engineer Field Troop, 1 x Army Air Corps Flight, 1 x Transport Sqn, 1 x Ordnance Company, REME Workshop, Field Ambulance detachment and an Intelligence section. The overall personnel total was probably in the region of 1500 men.

Northern Ireland

The military presence in support of the civilian authorities in Northern Ireland is controlled by HQ Northern Ireland (HQNI) which is located at Lisburn, just outside Belfast.

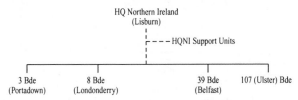

HQNI is responsible for counter terrorist operations in support of the Royal Ulster Constabulary (RUC). Under the operational command of these brigades (during late 1996) were:

                6 x Resident Infantry Battalions
                4 x Infantry Battalions on short 6 month tours
                1 x RA/RAC Regiments on short 6 month tours
                1 x Engineer Regiment
                1 x Royal Signals Regiment
                1 x Army Air Corps Regiment
                6 x Home Service Battalions of the Royal Irish Regiment
                1 x RLC Logistic Support Regiment
                1 x REME Workshop
                1 x Military Hospital manned by the Army Medical Services

1 x Prison Guard Force of Squadron/Battery strength

RAF: 1 x Wessex Squadron
 1 x Puma Squadron
 1 x RAF Regiment Squadron

Navy: 4 x Ships
 2 x Launches

During late 1996 there were approximately 12,500 regular soldiers and around 5,100 Royal Irish Regiment Home Service soldiers stationed in the Province (a high percentage of the regular soldiers on detachment from units either permanently stationed in Germany or the remainder of the UK Military Districts) making a total of approximately 17,600 soldiers available for security duties. In addition there are approximately 240 Royal Naval and 1,100 Royal Air Force personnel stationed in the Province.

Ulster Statistics

The last year for which comprehensive statistics are available was 1994.

	1994	1980
Deaths (Regular Army)	1	8
Deaths (Royal Irish)	2	8
Bombs neutralised	99	120
Explosives neutralised	1,688 kg	2,905 kg
Used in explosions	2,010 kg (est)	4,108 kg
Explosives found	1,285 kg	821 kg
Weapons found	264	203
Ammunition found	13,200 rounds	28,078 rounds

Overseas Garrisons

Brunei: 820 personnel
 1 x Gurkha Infantry Battalion
 Jungle Warfare Training School
 1 x Helicopter Flight

Cyprus: 2,807 personnel
 2 x Infantry Battalions
 1 x Engineer Support Squadron
 1 x Helicopter Flight
 1 x Signals Regiment

 With UNFICYP (United Nations Force in Cyprus)
 1 Roulement Regiment - Infantry Role.

Falkland
Islands: 800 men & women (approx)
 1 Infantry Company Group
 1 Engineer Squadron

	1 Signals Unit 1 Logistics Group Plus RAF and RN Units.
Gibraltar:	63 regular soldiers (approx) The Gibraltar Regiment (Reserve Unit)
Hong Kong:	1,770 personnel (Total includes RAF & RN) 1 x Infantry Battalion 1 x Helicopter Squadron (-)

Note: The garrison in Hong Kong closes following withdrawal on 30th June 1997.

Former Yugoslavia:	10,000 (Approx late 1996) 1 x Divisional Headquarters 1 x Armoured Brigade Command and Staff Elements of HQ ARRC Logistic and Support Units
Other Locations:	Approx 3,053 personnel in about 26 countries including Brunei, Botswana, Egypt, Gambia, Ghana, Mauritius, Namibia, Nigeria, Oman, Qatar, Saudi Arabia, Sudan, Swaziland, United Arab Emirates, Uganda, Zimbabwe, Kenya and Canada.

"The primary function of management is to create the chaos that only management can sort out. A secondary function is the expensive redecoration and refurnishing of offices, especially in times of the utmost financial stringency."

Theodore Dalrymple "The Spectator" 6 November 1993.

CHAPTER 3 - NATO

The United Kingdom is a member of the NATO (North Atlantic Treaty Organisation) and the majority of military operations are conducted in concert with the forces of NATO allies.

Following changes that took effect from 1 July 1993, NATO was reorganised from three into two major Commands. The first of these new commands is ACLANT (Allied Command Atlantic with headquarters at Norfolk, Virginia (USA) and the second is ACE (Allied Command Europe), with its headquarters at Mons in Belgium.

Operations in the NATO area in which the United Kingdom was a participant would almost certainly be as part of a NATO force under the command and control of Allied Command Europe (ACE). From October 1993 the Supreme Allied Commander Europe is General George A Joulwan of the United States Army. The current organisation of Allied Command Europe is as follows:

Allied Command Europe (ACE)

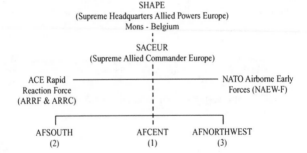

Notes:
(1) AFCENT - Allied Forces Central European Theatre with headquarters at Brunssum in the Netherlands and with overall responsibility for military operations in Central Europe. AFCENT is further subdivided into three subordinate commands - see next diagram.

(2) AFSOUTH - Allied Forces Southern Europe, with headquarters at Naples in Italy and responsible for military operations in the area of Turkey, Greece, Italy and is responsible for some aspects of operations in the Former Yugoslavia.

(3) AFNORTHWEST Allied Forces North-western Europe, with headquarters at High Wycombe in the UK. This new headquarters, was operational as from 1 July 1994 and is responsible for operations in Norway, the UK, and the maritime area between the two countries.

HQ AFNORTHWEST claims to be leaner and more efficient than its predecessor AFNORTH at Oslo in Norway, and became operational in July 1994. The headquarters is staffed by about 300 personnel, the majority of which are British, American and Norwegians, but Belgium, Canada, Denmark, Germany and the Netherlands are all represented.

Following reorganisation the composition of AFCENT is as follows:

Allied Forces Central European Theatre

AFCENT (3)
Commander-inChief
Allied Forces Central Europe
(CINCENT)
HQ Brunssum - Netherlands

AIRCENT (1)
Commander
Allied Air Forces
Central Europe
HQ Ramstein-Germany

LANDCENT (2)
Commander
Allied Land Forces
Central Europe
HQ Heidelberg-Germany

BALTAP
Commander
Allied Forces Baltic
Approaches
HQ Karup-Denmark

Note:
(1) AIRCENT is now responsible for all air forces in the AFCENT region.
(2) As an example, the LANDCENT HQ Staff consists of 159 Officers, 149 Non-commissioned Officers and Other Ranks and 15 NATO civilians - a total of 323 headquarters personnel. With Direct Support Units included the total is 744, and with the supporting Signal Unit the personnel figure approximately 2,500.
(3) The AFCENT operational area includes Northern Germany and Denmark, extending 800 kms to the south as far as the Swiss and Austrian borders.

The Allied Rapid Reaction Corps (ARRC)

NATO's latest strategic planning concept, which was initiated by the NATO Defence Planning Committee in May 1991 and confirmed during November 1991, called for the creation of Rapid Reaction Forces to meet the requirements of future challenges within the Alliance, whilst restructuring and reductions in national defence forces are going ahead. The ARRC provides the Supreme Allied Commander Europe with a multinational corps in which forward elements can be ready to deploy in Western Europe within 14 days.

Currently the ARRC trains for missions across the spectrum of operations from deterrence and crisis management to regional conflict. The formation has to be prepared to undertake Peace Support Operations - both peacekeeping and peacemaking. Belgium, Canada, Denmark, Germany, Greece, Italy, The Netherlands, Norway, Portugal, Spain, Turkey, the

United Kingdom and the United States all contribute to the Corps. Ten divisions are assigned to the ARRC and up to four of them could be placed under command for any specific operation. These divisions range from heavily armoured formations to lighter air portable units more suited to mountainous or difficult terrain. Some of these formations are National Divisions, some are Framework Divisions, where one nation takes the lead and another contributes, and two are Multinational Divisions where the member nations provide an equal share of the command, staff and combat forces.

The headquarters of the ARRC is fully multinational and is based at Rheindahlen, near Monchengladbach in Germany. The ARRC Commander is a British 3 Star General (from December 1994 - Lieutenant General Michael Walker), the Deputy Commander is an Italian 2 Star General and the Chief of Staff is a British 2 Star General. The Headquarters is approximately 1,000 strong, of which British personnel comprise about 50%. During October 1995 the Headquarters of the ARRC deployed outside Germany for the first time when the formation took part in Exercise Chinese Eye in Denmark. During early 1996 HQ ARRC deployed to Sarajevo in the Former Yugoslavia to command the NATO Implementation Force (IFOR)

Outline Composition of the ARRC (ACE Rapid Reaction Corps)

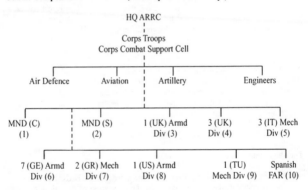

Notes: (1) MND(C) Multinational Division Central; (2) Multinational Division - South (3) Resident in Germany (4) Resident in the UK (5) IT - Italy (6) GE - Germany (7) GR Greece (8) US - United States (9) TU - Turkish (10) FAR - Rapid Action Force.

In peace, the headquarters of the ARRC and the two Multinational Divisions are under the command and control of SACEUR, but the remaining divisions and units only come under SACEUR's operational control after being deployed.

The operational organisation, composition and size of the ARRC would depend on the type of crisis, area of crisis, its political significance, and the capabilities and availability of lift assets, the distances to be covered and the infrastructure capabilities of the nation receiving assistance. It is considered that a four division ARRC would be the maximum employment structure.

The main British contribution to the ARRC is 1 (UK) Armoured Division that is stationed in Germany and there is also a considerable number of British personnel in both the ARRC Corps HQ and Corps Troops. In addition, in times of tension 3(UK) Div and 24 Airmobile Bde will move to the European mainland to take their place in the ARRC's order of battle. In total, we believe that if the need arises some 55,000 British Regular soldiers could be assigned to the ARRC (20,800 resident in Germany) together with a substantial numbers of Regular Army Reservists and formed TA Units.

Operations on the European mainland will generally be in support of the ARRC. This formation is the land component of the Allied Command Europe Rapid Reaction Forces and it is available for employment in support of SACEUR'S crisis management options whenever necessary. Its peacetime planning structure includes 10 divisions, plus corps troops from 12 NATO nations to allow a rapid response to a wide range of eventualities.

ARRC Groupings

Composition of the Multinational Division (Central) - MND(C)

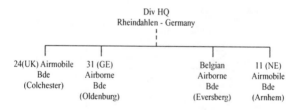

Composition of the Multinational Division (South) - MND(S)

Composition of the 1st (UK) Armoured Division

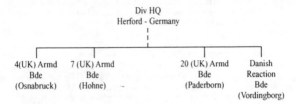

Div HQ
Herford - Germany

| 4(UK) Armd Bde (Osnabruck) | 7 (UK) Armd Bde (Hohne) | 20 (UK) Armd Bde (Paderborn) | Danish Reaction Bde (Vordingborg) |

Composition of the 3rd (UK) Mechanised Division

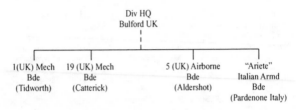

Div HQ
Bulford UK

| 1(UK) Mech Bde (Tidworth) | 19 (UK) Mech Bde (Catterick) | 5 (UK) Airborne Bde (Aldershot) | "Ariete" Italian Armd Bde (Pardenone Italy) |

Composition of the 3rd Italian Mechanised Division

Div HQ
Milan - Italy

| "Garibaldi" Mech Bde (Caserta) | "Julia" Mech Bde (Udine) | Portuguese Airborne Bde (Tancos) |

Composition of the 7th German Panzer Division

Div HQ
Dusseldorf - Germany

| 21 (GE) Armd Bde (Augustdorf) | 9 (GE) Armd Bde (Munster) |

Composition of the 2nd Greek Mechanised Division

Note: Other NATO nations could be invited to contribute a similar brigade to act as the third brigade within this divisional framework structure.

Composition of the 1st United States Armoured Division

Composition of the 1st Turkish Mechanised Division

Composition of the Spanish FAR Contingent (Fuerza De Accion Rapida)

Notes: The Spanish FAR equates roughly to the size of a conventional division.
1st (UK) Armoured Division is earmarked for operations within the NATO ARRC (Allied Rapid Reaction Corps), and in an emergency both 3 (UK) Mechanised Division and 24 Airmobile Brigade would be expected to move from their bases in the UK to the European

mainland, to reinforce the NATO formations of which they are a part.

British Forces in Bosnia

UK Forces have been deployed in the Former Yugoslavia since 1992. Initially these forces were under command of the United Nations Protection Force (UNPROFOR) and from 20th December 1995 these forces have been under the command of the NATO Implementation Force (IFOR). At the height of the UNPROFOR commitment there were approximately 5,000 British troops serving with the force. Towards the end of 1996 British Forces committed to IFOR numbered just over 10,000, approximately 10 per cent of the Army's effective strength. The cost of the British involvement in the Former Yugoslavia was £300 million during the calendar year 1996.

Since the first deployment to the Former Yugoslavia in 1992 eleven British members of the British forces have been killed as a result of hostile action and a further 14 have died as a result of gunshot wounds or vehicle accidents (figure correct up to November 1996).

The IFOR mandate agreed at Dayton, Ohio on the 21st November 1995 includes:

(1) Boundary demarcation between the Federation of Bosnian Croats and Muslims and the Republic Srpska (including areas to be transferred from one entity to another).
(2) Separation of the forces of the former warring factions and the supervision of their withdrawal to barracks. (3) Deployment of a multinational force to implement the military aspects of the above arrangements. (4) To implement confidence and security building measures to promote regional stability. (5) To establish a constitution for Bosnia & Herzegovina with a central government but separate administrations for the Federation and the Republic Srpska. (6) Ensuring elections throughout Bosnia under the supervision of the OSCE (Organisation for Security and Cooperation in Europe). (7) Observance of the rights of refugees and displaced persons and the maintenance of human rights in general. (8) Implementation of the non-military aspects of the Peace Agreement. (9) Establishment by the UN of an International Police Task Force. Between December 1995 and January 1996 approximately 55,000 IFOR personnel deployed to the Former Yugoslavia under the following command arrangements:

IFOR Command Structure

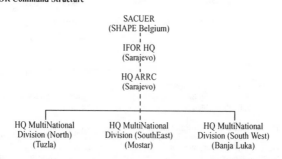

SACUER
(SHAPE Belgium)

IFOR HQ
(Sarajevo)

HQ ARRC
(Sarajevo)

HQ MultiNational Division (North) (Tuzla) — HQ MultiNational Division (SouthEast) (Mostar) — HQ MultiNational Division (South West) (Banja Luka)

Notes:

(1) HQ MND(N) or HQ MultiNational Division (North) were commanded by a US General and included US, Russian, Turkish and Nordic units.

(2) HQ MND(SE) or HQ MultiNational Division (South East) was commanded by a French General and includes French, Spanish and Italian Units.

(3) HQ MND(SW) or HQ MultiNational Division (South West) was commanded by a British General.

Outline Organisation HQ MultiNational Division (South West)

HQ MND (SW) was based upon the HQ of 3 (UK) Div for the first half of 1996 and of HQ 1 (UK) Armd Div during the latter half of the year.

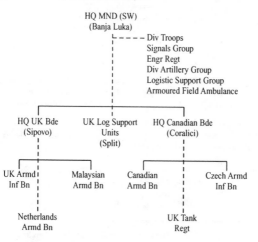

Logistic Support

National IFOR contingents provide their own logistic support. Of the mid 1996 total of just over 10,000 UK personnel in theatre, about 3,000 were involved in logistical support. The major support base is on the Adriatic coast at the port of Split in Croatia and at the height of the operation the Royal Logistic Corps (RLC) was handling about 1,000 requests for supplies per day. Delivery of supplies from Split to the forward UK units had accounted for almost 3 million kilometres of road distance run by RLC vehicles by mid 1996.

During mid 1996 there were over 7,500 vehicles in use by UK forces in the theatre, of which 1,500 were Land Rovers.

The Future

On the 18th November 1996 NATO Foreign Ministers meeting in Brussels decided that after December 1996 a new NATO Stabilisation Force of approximately 30,000 personnel, roughly half of the strength of IFOR would remain in the Former Yugoslavia until 1998. The command arrangements for the force are similar to the previous arrangements but divisional commands have been replaced by large brigades, each of which is commanded by a two star general (in the case of the UK, a major general). The new force will be known as SFOR

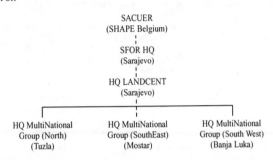

SACUER
(SHAPE Belgium)

SFOR HQ
(Sarajevo)

HQ LANDCENT
(Sarajevo)

HQ MultiNational Group (North) (Tuzla) — HQ MultiNational Group (SouthEast) (Mostar) — HQ MultiNational Group (South West) (Banja Luka)

The Multi National Group (South West) will be commanded by the headquarters of 20 Armoured Bde (detached from 1 (UK) Armoured Division in Germany) until mid 1997 when it will be replaced by another Brigade headquarters.

SFOR - UK Group

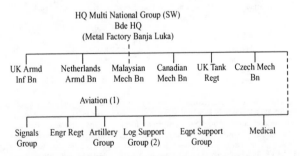

HQ Multi National Group (SW)
Bde HQ
(Metal Factory Banja Luka)

UK Armd Inf Bn — Netherlands Armd Bn — Malaysian Mech Bn — Canadian Mech Bn — UK Tank Regt — Czech Mech Bn

Aviation (1)

Signals Group — Engr Regt — Artillery Group — Log Support Group (2) — Eqpt Support Group — Medical

Notes: (1) Aviation will probably include 1 x AAC Sqn, 1 x RAF Support Helicopter detachment with at least 2 x Chinook and possibly 4 x Sea Kings from the Fleet Air Arm. (2) Each of the national contingents is responsible for the majority of its own logistic support. The headquarters of the UK Logistic group will remain in Split

CHAPTER 4 - The Household Cavalry and the Royal Armoured Corps

Ambitious Infantry Major "Do you know that even in 1996 the British Army has more horses than helicopters?".

Laid Back Cavalry Subaltern "Quite right too!"

Overheard in the Officers Mess of the Combined Arms Training Centre.

The Household Cavalry and The Royal Armoured Corps (RAC) provide the tank force and armoured reconnaissance component of the British Army.

The Household Cavalry consists of 2 regiments, the first of these being the Household Cavalry Mounted Regiment, stationed in London and with a primary task as a ceremonial unit providing escorts etc for state occasions. The second is the Household Cavalry Regiment currently (1997) employed as an armoured reconnaissance regiment, but in the longer term could be equipped as a main battle tank regiment as units are rotated through different roles.

The RAC is composed of 10 regular regiments and five TA Yeomanry Regiments. Apart from the Royal Tank Regiment, which was formed in the First World War with the specific task of fighting in armoured vehicles, the regular element of the RAC is provided by the Regiments which formed the cavalry element of the pre-mechanised era. Of the 5 TA Yeomanry regiments one is an armoured reconnaissance regiment and the remaining four are equipped as national defence reconnaissance regiments.

Of the 11 regular regiments equipped with armoured vehicles, 7 are stationed in Germany with 1 (UK) Armoured Division, and of these 6 are equipped with Challenger 1/2 main battle tanks, and the 7th is an armoured reconnaissance regiment equipped with a mix of Scimitar, Striker and Spartan.

In the UK there are 2 regular armoured regiments equipped with Challenger MBT stationed in Tidworth and Catterick. Both of these regiments are under the operational command of 3 (UK) Division that has a role in support of the ARRC. There is also 1 regular armoured reconnaissance regiment stationed in the UK also under the operational command of 3 (UK) Division. An armoured training regiment is based at the RAC Training Centre located at Bovington in Dorset.

The Territorial Army has 5 Yeomanry Regiments and an independent squadron. These units provide 1 armoured reconnaissance regiment for the reinforcement of the ARRC and 4 national defence regiments with a reconnaissance role.

During 1994 the UK MOD announced the formation of the British Army's first Nuclear, Biological and Chemical Defence Regiment (NBC). During the period 1995 to 1997 one of the Territorial Army's Yeomanry Regiments - The Royal Yeomanry converted from its previous role as a national defence reconnaissance regiment. In the longer term the Royal Yeomanry will support all existing plans for NBC defence throughout the British Army and could be used to support action following radiological accidents and chemical spills. The core element of this new regiment is the 11 x Fuchs reconnaissance vehicles that were supplied to the British Army during the Gulf War. These 11 vehicles form one squadron, with another two squadrons mounted in wheeled vehicles. All three squadrons are equipped with the joint US/ UK Integrated Biological Detection System (IBDS) the British version of which was developed at the Chemical Defence

Establishment at Porton Down in Wiltshire.

In July 1991 the UK MOD announced the purchase of 127 Vickers Defence Systems (VDS) Challenger 2 main battle tanks. Vickers Defence Systems won the £500 million contract against intense competition from the French Leclerc, German Leopard 2 (Improved) and the US M1A2 Abrams. The Challenger 2 MBT unit price is believed to have been in the region of £2.5 million and defence industry sources suggest that this price was considerably cheaper than that of the French Leclerc or the German Leopard 2. In July 1994 the UK Secretary of State for Defence announced the purchase of a further 259 Challenger 2 bringing the total to 386, and allowing for the complete UK MBT fleet to be upgraded to the Challenger 2 standard.

At the same time it was announced that in future British armoured regiments operating Challenger 2 MBT would reduce from regiments with 50 main battle tanks organised in four squadrons to a new organisation of 38 tanks with three squadrons. This will allow for six Challenger 2 regiments in Germany, two in the UK, a training regiment at Bovington and a war maintenance reserve (WMR) of approximately 50 tanks.

The Royal Scots Dragoon Guards took delivery of the first production models of the Challenger 2 in July 1994 and by January 1997 our estimate is that about 40 had been delivered. In early 1996 VDS announced that problems had been identified in the Challenger 2 turret systems and that these problems were responsible for a delay in the tank's full commissioning into service. The company stated that there had been some integration and quality control problems with turret sub-systems, 80 per cent of which had been purchased from outside contractors. The exact details of these problems were not revealed but VDS has recently stated that the problems had been overcome, tested on the vehicles and implemented. Unlike many other MBT programmes, no software problems have been reported on Challenger 2 and the chassis and 120 mm L30 rifled gun are believed to be problem free.

British armoured forces appear to be emerging from a period where their utility has been questioned and although the value of armour has once again been proven during the Gulf War and recent operations in Bosnia, at the time of writing the long term future of the MBT in its present form remains uncertain, and although the most dedicated armoured soldier will still insist that the tank is the most effective anti-tank weapon on the battlefield, others would disagree. The supremacy of armour on the modern battlefield continues to be challenged by anti-tank helicopters such as the Russian Havoc and US Apache. Helicopters which travel at speeds of up to 300 kph, carrying missiles with ranges of up to 5,000+ metres, threaten the flanks of armoured formations that might have a top speed of 80 kph and effective gun ranges of 2,000 metres. On the ground the infantry can defend themselves with portable missile systems such as the Soviet Spigot , European Milan and US TOW, while third generation fire and forget weapons such as Trigat that will shortly enter service will further enhance defences. Missiles such as these, with ranges in excess of 2,000 metres, and the ability to penetrate over 350 mm of armour, contribute to making the modern battlefield a lethal environment for armour.

Syrian experience in the Lebanon during the 1982 war, when over 400 Soviet manufactured Syrian T-62 and T-72's were destroyed by the Israelis using a combination of aircraft, attack helicopters and ground based TOW missiles, would serve to underline this belief. We feel that recent experience in the Gulf has added more weight to the argument in favour of the attack helicopter and do not believe that the current trend in uparmouring main battle tanks will do anything more than obtain a short breathing space for armour, before the next round of improvements in anti-tank weapons appear.

The correct answer to this problem would be to have large numbers of MBT, attack helicopters and ground based anti-armour systems, but it is unrealistic to expect that a small nation with expensive world-wide commitments can afford this luxury. Up to now the British defence establishment appears to have made armour its highest priority, but there are now clear signs which suggest that in the longer term thinking may be slowly moving in the direction of a heliborne missile anti-tank defensive system. We see the establishment of 24 Airmobile Brigade and the creation of a sixth Army Air Corps Regiment as evidence of a gradual shift in emphasis in favour of the anti-tank helicopter solution.

However, we do not believe that the Main Battle Tank is redundant on the modern battlefield. Armour will almost certainly have a major military role to play for many years to come and we predict that during the early part of the next century armoured formations will remain an essential part of any military force. We are at the beginning of a time of great military change, and the only military certainty that we can see on the horizon is for the continuing need to hold or capture ground. This requirement alone should ensure the survival of armoured formations, but the size of these formations will almost certainly be greatly reduced, and organisations and tactics could be very different from those in use today. It must also be said that although main battle tanks are slow in comparison with attack helicopters and lack the range of Trigat or Hellfire missiles, when the weather is bad and attack helicopters cannot fly, the tanks will continue to be available and capable of carrying out their mission. Recent defensive measures such as lasers that destroy incoming missiles, multispectral smoke that confuses missile guidance systems and goalkeeper type machine guns linked to close radar systems, capable of destroying anti-tank missiles during the last 5 seconds of flight may well provide a significant defensive boost for the tank of the future, and improve the longer term prospects for armour on the battlefield.

For the longer term the "crystal ball" appears to be clearing a little. While we are reasonably certain of a reduction in the numbers of main battle tanks in most national inventories, the manoeuvrable light armoured vehicle, capable of operating in a 24 hour battlefield scenario and possibly acting as a command and control unit (electronic mother station/ digital relay) for smaller mobile sub units is beginning to look like a priority option. The UK Verdi and Tracer programmes appear to be coming together to provide such an option and digitisation of the future battlefield may well see large numbers of these vehicles in service during the early part of the new century.

Armoured Regiment Wiring Diagram

The following diagram shows the current structure of an Armoured Regiment equipped with Challenger 1. Regiments equipped with Challenger 2 will only have three sabre squadrons and a total of 38 tanks.

Armoured Regiment

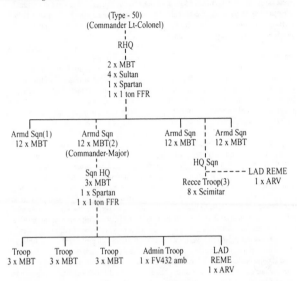

Totals: 50 x MBT (Challenger 1), 8 x Scimitar, 5 x ARV, 558 men.

Notes:

(1) Armoured Squadron;

(2) Main Battle Tank;

(3) We believe that this recce troop of 8 x Scimitar is normally held in HQ Sqn but on operations comes under the direct control of the commanding officer;

(4) The basic building brick of the Tank Regiment is the Tank Troop of 12 men and three tanks. The commander of this troop will probably be a Lt or 2/Lt aged between 20 or 23 and the second-in-command will usually be a sergeant who commands his own tank. The remaining tank in the troop will be commanded by a senior corporal;

(5) A Challenger tank has a crew of 4 - Commander, Driver, Gunner and Loader/Operator.

Armoured Reconnaissance Regiment
(Commander - Lt-Colonel)

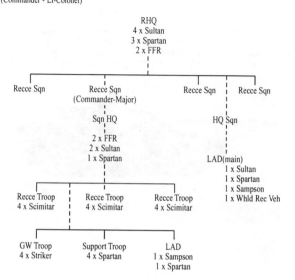

Totals: 48 x Scimitar, 16 x Striker, 20 x Spartan, Approx 600 men.

At the beginning of 1997 there are 2 regular armoured reconnaissance regiments in the British Order of Battle. One is in Germany with 1(UK) Armd Div and the other in the UK with 3(UK) Div. Both of these recce regiments have an organisation based on the diagram shown above. TA Recce regiments based inthe UK with a national defence role are equipped with open Land Rovers.

Amoured reconnaissance regiments are usually under the direct command of a divisional headquarters and their more usual task in a defensive scenario is to identify the direction and strength of the enemy thrusts, impose maximum delay and damage while allowing main forces to manoeuvre to combat the threat. They would be assisted in such a task by anti-tank helicopters, long range anti-tank missile systems such as Swingfire, and for the action to be successful every engagement will need to be planned as an ambush. In support will be the indirect fire guns of the divisional artillery, and an air defended area (ADA) maintained by Rapier and Javelin air defence missiles.

The basic task of all of these recce regiments is to obtain accurate information about the enemy and ensure that it is passed back through the chain of command as quickly as possible.

Fv 4030/4 Challenger 1

(379 in Operational Service on 1 Jan 1997 - being replaced by Challenger 2). Armament 1 x 120 mm L11A7 gun: 2 x 7.62 Machine Guns: 2 x 5 barrel smoke dischargers: Engine Rolls-Royce CV12: Ammunition Capacity 44 rounds of 120mm: 6000 rounds of 7.62 mm: Engine Power 1,200 bhp at 2,300 rpm: Engine Capacity 26.1 litres: Max Road Speed 56kph: Weight loaded 62,000kg: Length Hull 9.87m: Length Gun Forward 11.55m: Height 3.04m: Width 3.42m: Ground Clearance O.5m: Crew 4: Ground Pressure 0.96 kg/cm2: Fording Depth (no prep) 1.07m.

Produced by the Royal Ordnance Factory in Leeds the first Challenger 1's were delivered to the British Army in 1983.

Challenger 1 is a development of the Centurion/Chieftain line which was modified to produce the Shir/Iran 2 originally planned for service with the Iranian forces. After the Iranian Revolution the Shir Iran 2 project was taken over by the British Army and the end result was Challenger later re-designated as Challenger 1.

The main differences between Challenger 1 and its predecessor Chieftain (the MBT that it replaced) were in the engine and armour. The Challenger engine, which produces 1,200bhp at 2,300rpm was far more powerful than the Chieftain engine, and the Chobham Armour carried is believed to give protection from almost all types of anti-tank weapon. Chobham armour is thought to consist of several layers of nylon micromesh, bonded on both sides by sheets of titanium alloy, in addition to several other layers of specialised armour and ceramics. Challenger 1 is believed to have cost about £2 million per vehicle at 1987 prices.

The main armament on all Challenger 1's has been upgraded by the installation of the L30 CHARM gun. In addition to firing the existing range of ammunition, this gun fires a new armour piercing fin stabilised discarding sabot round with a depleted uranium warhead, which should be able to defeat the armour on all known MBT's. An additional improvement is the ACTAS (Active Cupola Target Acquisition System) which has been retrofitted to all Challenger 1's. This system permits the use of the commander's cupola for target acquisition and designation to the gunner. We would expect to see Challenger 1 phased out and replaced by Challenger 2 by the end of the decade.

The only nation known to be operating Challenger 1 other than the UK is Jordan, where the 274 tanks in service are known as Khalid. The UK also operates approximately 77 Challenger 1 ARV's and 16 Challenger 1 driver training tanks.

Challenger 2

(386 Challenger 2 on Order probably about 40 delivered by 1 Jan 1997) Crew 4; Length Gun Forward 11.55m; Hull Length 8.32m; Height to Turret Roof 2.49m; Width 3.52m; Ground Clearance 0.50m; Combat Weight 62,500 kgs; Main Armament 1 x 120mm L30 CHARM Gun; Ammunition Carried 52 rounds APFSDS, HESH, Smoke, DU; Secondary Armament Co-axial 7.62mm MG; 7.62mm GPMG Turret Mounted for Air Defence; Ammunition Carried 4000 rounds 7.62mm; Engine CV12TCA 12 cylinder Auxiliary Engine Perkins 4.108 4 - stroke diesel; Gearbox TN54 epicyclic - 6 forward gears and 2 reverse; Road Speed 56 kph; Cross Country Speed 40 kph; Fuel Capacity 1,797 litres.

In July 1991 the UK MOD announced an order for 127 Challenger 2 MBT and 13 driver training tanks. This initial order was followed in July 1994 by a further contract for 259 vehicles to make a total of 386. This will be enough to equip 8 regiments with the vehicle and allow 82 tanks for training and reserve. A regiment will have 38 tanks in three squadrons. Challenger 2 is manufactured by Vickers Defence Systems and production will be undertaken at their factories in Newcastle-Upon-Tyne and Leeds. At 1995 prices Challenger 2 is believed to cost £2.5 million per vehicle.

Challenger 2 completed its Reliability Growth Trial (RGT) in 1994 and during these trials 3 vehicles were tested over a total of about 285 battlefield days. For the purposes of the trial a battlefield day consisted of:

> 27 kms of Road Travel
> 33 kms of Cross Country Travel
> Firing 34 Main Armament Rounds
> Firing 1,000 7.62mm MG rounds
> 16 Hours of Weapon Systems Operation
> 10 Hours of Main Engine Idling
> 3.5 Hours of Main Engine Running Mobile

Although the hull and automotive parts of the Challenger 2 are based upon that of its predecessor Challenger 1, the new tank incorporates over 150 improvements aimed at increasing reliability and maintainability. The whole of the Challenger 2 turret is of a totally new design and the vehicle has a crew of four; commander, gunner, loader/signaller and driver. The 120mm rifled Royal

Ordnance L30 gun fies all current tank ammunition plus th new depleted uranium (D) round with a stick charge propellant system.

The design of the turret incorporates several of the significant features that Vickers had developed for its Mk 7 MBT (a Vickers turret on a Leopard 2 chassis). The central feature is an entirely new fire control system based on the Ballistic Control System developed by Computing Devices Company (Canada) for the US Army's M1A1 MBT. This second generation computer incorporates dual 32bit processors with a MIL STD1553B databus and has sufficient growth potential to accept Battlefield Information Control System (BICS) functions and navigation aids (a GPS satnav system). The armour is an uprated version of Challenger 1's Chobham armour.

The first production models of the Challenger 2 were taken into service by the Royal Scots Dragoon Guards in mid 1994. The actual in service date (ISD) for the vehicle is December 1996 (probably subject to some slippage) and we would expect to see all 386 Challenger 2's in service with the British Army by the end of the decade.

The only export order so far is an Omani order for 18 x Challenger 2 MBTs, 2 x Driver Training Vehicles and 4 x Challenger Armoured Repair and Recovery Vehicles signed during 1993. However, Vickers Defence Systems have high hopes for the vehicle in the remainder of the world market during the next ten years.

Sabre

As part of the UK MoDs CVR(T) rationalisation programme both the tracked Scorpion with its 76mm gun and the wheeled Fox with its 30mm Rarden Cannon were withdrawn from service and a hybrid vehicle Sabre produced. Essentially Sabre consists of the Scorpion chassis fitted with the turret of a Fox.

In addition to the installation of the manually operated two man Fox turret, extensive modifications have ben carried out by 34 BaseWorkshops at Donnington. These modifications include redesigned smoke grenade dischargers, replacement of the 7.62 MG with a 7.62mm Chain Gun, new light clusters and additional side bins. Domed hatches have also improved headroom for both commander and gunner.

We believe that about 104 Sabre vehicle will be introduced into service and that the vehicle could replace Scimitar in the Recce elements of both tank and armoured reconnaissance regiments.

Fv 102 Striker

(Approx 68 in service) Armament 10 x Swingfire Missiles: 1 x 7.62mm Machine Gun: 2 x 4 barrel smoke dischargers: Engine Jaguar J 60 No.1 Mark 100B: Engine Power 190bhp: Fuel Capacity 350 litres: Max Road Speed 80kph: Road Range 483km: Length 4.8m: Height 2.2m: Width 2.2m: Ground Clearance 0.35m: Ammunition Capacity 3,000 rounds 7.62: Main Armament Traverse 53 degrees left, 55 degrees right.

Striker is one of the famiy of the CR(T) vehicles (Combat Vehicle Reconnaissance Tracked) which includes Spartan, Sultan, Samaritan and Scorpion. Striker carries 10 Swingfire anti-tank missiles with a range of up to 4,000 metres. Five of these missiles are carried in bins on top of the vehicle, which can be lowered when the system is not expected to be in action. One significant drawback to the system is the reload operation, which requires a crewman to reload the missile bins from outside the vehicle. There is also a separated sight available which enables the launch vehicle to be hidden in dead ground, and the operator to fire and control the flight of the missile from a position up to 10m away from the launch vehicle.

Swingfire (cost per missile 7,500) is due for replacement by Trigat LR towards the end of the decade.

The striker system enables a fast, hard hitting anti-tank missile launch platform to keep up with the latest MBTs. Striker is to be found in the armoured reconnaissance regiment which has a troop of four vehicles in each of its three recce squadrons.

Swingfire Data

Type - Anti Tank Guided Missile; Wire Guided; Command to line of sight: Length of Missile 1.06m: Body Diameter 37.3cm: Warhead Hollow Charge HE: Propellant Solid Fuel: Weight of Missile 37kg: Minimum Range 150m: Maximum Range 4,000m.

Trigat LR

Range 5000+ metres: Missile Weight 20 kgs.

Trigat is a European collaborative programme which is designed to produce a family of medium and long range, anti tank missiles for the 1990s and beyond. Trigat LR (Long Range) will be the missile that replaces Swingfire in British Service.

Trigat LR is believed to be designed for heliborne or tank destroyer type launch platforms and will have a full fire and forget capability. Present plans are thought to include a launch platform with a raised gantry, which could be elevated to a height of about 6 metres and produce a dramatic increase in the operators field of fire.

We believe that Trigat LR will cost over £50,000 per missile and if this initial estimate is correct, there is little doubt that practice firings will not be an everyday occurrence. There is much confusion regarding the UK's future involvement in the Trigat LR programme. The UK MOD states that the development programme is continuing on a revised basis, consistent with the UK's priorities. We would be surprised if Trigat LR is in service before the end of the decade.

The three partners in the Trigat LR project are France, Germany and the UK with the manufacturer being the Euromissile Dynamics Group. A number of other European Union nations are showing interest in the system.

Fv 107 Scimitar

(300) in service). Armament 1 x 30mm Rarden L21 Gun: 1 x 7.62mm Machine Gun: 2 x 4 barrel smoke dischargers: Engine Jaguar J60 No.1 Mark 100B: Engine Power 190bhp: Fuel Capacity 423 litres: Max Road Speed 80kph: Weight loaded 7,750kg: Length 4.9m: Height 2.096m: Width 2.2m: Ground Clearance 0.35m: Road Range 644km: Crew 3: Ammunition Capacity 30mm - 160 rounds; 7.62mm - 3,000 rounds: Main Armament Elevation - 10 degrees to + 35 degrees.

Very much the same vehicle as the Scorpion, but with a different gun, the Scimitar is the mainstay of the Armoured Recce Regiment. The Scimitar is an ideal recce vehicle, mobile and fast with good communications and excellent viewing equipment. Recce Platoons belonging to Infantry Battalions stationed in Germany are also equipped with Scimitar.

Fuchs

(11 In Service) Road Range 800 kms; Crew 2; Operational Weight 17,000 kg; Length 6.83m; Width 2.98m; Height 2.30m; Road Speed 105 kph; Engine Mercedes-Benz Model OM-402A V-8 liquid cooled diesel; Armament 1 x 7.62mm MG; 6 x Smoke Dischargers.

Manufactured by the German company ThyssenHenschel as the Transporter Panzer 1 this is an amphibious vehicle with a water speed of 10 kph. During the Gulf War the UK purchased 11 of the NBC Reconnaissance version of this vehicle and they will now become the core element of the UK's Nuclear, Biological and Chemical Defence Regiment being formed by the RoyalYeomanry. For NBC Defence work the vehicles will be equipped with the joint US/UK Integrated Biological Detection System (IBDS), the British version of which is currently under development at the Chemical Defence Establishment at Porton Down in Wiltshire.

Approximately 1,000 Transporter Panzer 1 vehicles are in service with the German Army in 7 basic roles. The NBC version is also in service with the USA (60), Israel (8), Turkey (4) and the Netherlands (6).

Challenger Armoured Repair and Recovery Vehicle (ARRV)

(80 In Service) Crew 3; Length 9.59m; Operating Width 3.62m; Height 3.005m; Ground Clearance 0.5m; Combat Weight 62, 000kg; Max Road Speed 59 kph; Cross Country Speed 35 kph; Fording 1.07m; Trench Crossing 2.3m; Crane - Max Lift 6,500kg at 4.9m reach; Engine Perkins CV12 TCA 1200 26.1 V-12 direct injection 4-stroke diesel.
Between 1988 and 1990 the British Army ordered 80 Challenger ARRV (Rhino) in two batches and the contract was completed wit the last vehicles bought into service during 1983. A 50 tank Challenger 1 Regiment has 5 x ARRV, one with each sabre squadron and one with the REME Light Aid Detachment (LAD). This total will probably fall to four in the new 38 tank Challenger 2 Regiment.

The vehicle has a crew of three plus additional space in a separate compartment for another two REME fitters. The vehicle is fitted with two winches (main and auxiliary) plus an Atlas hydraulically operated crane capable of lifting a complete Challenger 2 powerpack. The front dozer blade can be used as a stabiliser blade for the crane or as a simple earth anchor.

Chieftain ARRV's are believed to have been withdrawn from service.

TRACER

Under current plans, the British Army, RAF Regiment and Royal Marines will be equipped with an entirely new family of light armoured vehicles early in the next century. UK design teams are currently working on a modular/family concept that could replace the range of light armoured vehicles that include Scorpion Striker, Scimitar, Sultan, Spartan, Sampson, Fox and Ferret.

FFLAV (Future Family of Light Armoured Vehicles) was originally conceived to cover the weight range from approximately 5 to 25 tons, with the majority of the heavier vehicles being tracked and the remainder wheeled. To reduce costs, plans were made to use existing, in-production automotive components, many of which could be purchased off the shelf. Such a design policy will almost certainly reduce the cost per vehicle, and make the series attractive in the export market. In addition many vehicles which are currently soft skinned (unarmoured), such as command and communications vehicles were included in the concept to reduce vulnerability to small arms fire, shell splinters, NBC agents etc.

Following the reduction in the threat, the FFLAV programme has been turned into the LAVS (Light Armoured Vehicle Strategy) which is the programme umbrella for TRACER (Tactical Reconnaissance Armoured Combat Equipment Requirement). TRACER was officially launched in a presentation to industry in September 1992 and the programme will seek to rectify the defects in the CVR(T) Series which were described in the 1992 Statements on the Defence Estimates as follows:-

"The CVR(T) light armoured reconnaissance vehicles were not well suited to fast-moving offensive operations in open country and their employment was constrained by a relative lack of mobility, protection and older generation optics". In June 1993 three consortia were awarded a one-year contract for a feasibility study and report on the TRACER requirement. These three consortia were Royal Ordnance teamed with Alvis, GEC Marconi's Radar and Control Systems teamed with GKN defence and Vickers Defence Systems teamed with Shorts, Siemens Plessey, Teledyne and Texas Instruments. These feasibility studies were completed in April 1994, and following analysis of the studies plus contributions from other MOD Departments, it is looking likely that TRACER could be a tracked vehicle weighing around 20 tonnes and armed with a 45 mm CTA (Cased Telescoped Ammunition) weapon, anti-tank guided missiles and a sophisticated array of sensors.

An amended TRACER staff requirement was believed to have been issued at the end of 1996. Two contractors are probably going to be chosen for a competitive project definition phase running from 1997-99, with 2006 as the projected in-service date.

We would expect TRACER type vehicles to take on a wide variety of roles, which could include armoured personnel carriers (to replace AFV 432's not included in the Warrior replacement programme) armoured ambulance, communications, reconnaissance, repair and recovery. We also expect there to be a requirement for a simple tank destroyer type vehicle design to mount Trigat LR, and tracked vehicle launch platforms for Rapier 2000. In the initial stages of the project only a basic scout and utility version of the vehicle are planned.

We believe that current political developments in Europe, coupled with the reductions in British Forces will reduce the size of this potential TRACER market to approx 750 units (250 reconnaissance and 500 utility) that the only way to achieve volume sales will be within the European Defence Market. Teaming arrangements by major British defence firms such as Alvis, GKN and Vickers will be necessary to penetrate these markets, and there are already reports of European firms such as Krauss Maffei, Thyssen Henschel, Renault, Panard and Oto Melara becoming involved with British manufacturers.

VERDI

VERDI (Vehicle Electronics Research Defence Initiative) is the title for a concept demonstration vehicle in a co-operative programme between the UK MOD, DRA and UK industry. The programme is now at the VERDI II stage where a two man crew operate a modified Warrior using computers, integrated data bases, sensors, weapon systems and electronic displays to fight the vehicle in a closed down, comfortable and ergonomic environment. VERDI gives a glimpse of the armoured vehicle of the future and during a recent exercise a VERDI vehicle was able to sit inside a wood, extend a surveillance mast above the trees and transmit real time images back to a command post via a data link.

We would expect that experience gained in the VERDI programme will have a major impact on the type of vehicle finally adopted in the TRACER programme. The final TRACER Reconnaissance vehicle will almost certainly have some resemblance to the VERDI II vehicle.

MARDI

The first MARDI (Mobile Advanced Robotics Defence Initiative) vehicles were involved in field trials during 1993 on Salisbury Plain when a command centre was set up to control an unmanned Streaker vehicle over distances of up to 7 kms. The Streaker vehicle was fitted with a reconnaissance pod containing a TV camera, thermal imager, laser rangefinder and acoustic sensors and can be used for a number of missions including battlefield surveillance, artillery observation and target acquisition.

MARDI also serves as a pointer towards the future, and within twenty years unmanned vehicles datalinked to remote controllers are almost certainly going to be very common on any future battlefield.

CHAPTER 5 - INFANTRY

"They'll drink every hour of the daylight and poach every hour of dark.
It's the sport not the rabbits they're after. We've plenty of game in the park.
Don't hang them or cut off their fingers. That's wasteful as well as unkind.
For a hard bitten, South-country poacher makes the best man-at-arms you can find".

Advice from the dying Norman Baron to his son.- Rudyard Kipling - Norman & Saxon.

Regiments and Battalions

The British Infantry is based on the well tried and tested Regimental System; validated regularly on operational deployment, it is based on Regiments some which are comprised of one regular battalion and one TA battalion, and others that have two or three battalions and a corresponding number of TA battalions. Regiments are grouped together within administrative Divisions which in this sense are not field formations but historical groupings based on recruiting geography.

The Division of Infantry is an organisation that is responsible for all aspects of military administration, from recruiting, manning and promotions for individuals in the regiments under its wing, to the longer term planning required to ensure continuity and cohesion. Divisions of Infantry have no operational command over their regiments, and should not be confused with the operational divisions such as 1(UK) Armd Div and 3(UK) Div.

The Divisions of Infantry are as follows:

The Guards Division	- 5 regular battalions
The Scottish Division	- 6 regular battalions
The Queen's Division	- 6 regular battalions
The King's Division	- 6 regular battalions
The Prince of Wales Division	- 7 regular battalions
The Light Division	- 4 regular battalions

Not administered by Divisions of Infantry but operting under thir own administrative arrangements are the following:

The Parachute Regiment	- 3 regular battalions
The Brigade of Gurkhas	- 2 regular battalions
The Royal Irish Regiment	- 1 regular battalion

TA battalions are under the administrative command of the following:

The Guards Division	- Nil
The Scottish Division	- 5 TA battalions
The Queen's Division	- 8 TA battalions
The King's Division	- 6 TA battalions
The Prince of Wales Division	- 6 TA battalions
The Light Division	- 6 TA battalions
The Parachute Regiment	- 2 TA battalions
The Royal Irish Regiment	- 1 TA battalion

In total the British Army has 40 regular battalions available for service and this total combined with the 34 TA battalions (including 4 fire support battalions) could give a mobilisation strength of 74 infantry battalions.

Outside the above listed Regiments are three companies of guardsmen each of 110 men, who are provided to supplement the Household Division Regiments while on public duties in London, to allow them to continue to carry out normal training on roulement from guard duties. Gibraltar also has its own single battalion of the Gibraltar Regiment comprising one Regular and two TA companies.

At the beginning of 1997 the infantry will be located as follows:

United Kingdom	31	bns (6 Resident in Northern Ireland)
Germany	6	bns
Cyprus	2	bns
Hong Kong	1	bn (from UK and to be withdrawn in mid 1997)
Brunei	1	bn (Gurkha)
Falkland Islands	1	Company Group on detachment
Bosnia	1	bn on detachment from Germany

As explained previously it would be most unusual for the Infantry to fight as battalion units especially in armoured or mechanised formations. The HQ of an infantry battalion will generally be the HQ of a battle group, and the force will be provided with armour, artillery, engineers and possibly aviation to enable it to become a balanced all arms grouping.

Types of Infantry Battalions

Armoured Infantry Battalion	- Equipped with Warrior AFV.
Mechanised Infantry Battalion	- Equipped with Saxon APC.
Light Role Infantry Battalion	- Equipped for General Service.

The other types of battalion are:

Airmobile Infantry Battalion - A battalion with three rifle companies adapted for use with 24 Airmobile Brigade. Total strength is 680 all ranks.

Parachute Battalion - There are three parachute battalions of which two serve with 5 Airborne Brigade at any one time. Total Strength is 634 men.

AMF(L) Battalion - This Battalion is drawn from the Joint Rapid Deployment Force Battalions and has 679 men.

Gurkha Infantry Battalion -Equipped as a light role Battalion.

TA Infantry Battalion - Scaled and equipped to suit the special requirements of the Territorial Army, generally speaking these battalions have three rifle companies.

TA Fire Support Battalion - A new structure with two heavy weapons companies. Total personnel strength will be 336.

Numbers of Battalions in Specific Roles

Infantry Bn (Armd)	- 8
Infantry Bn (Mech)	- 4
Infantry Bn (Airmob)	- 2
Infantry Bn (Light Role)	- 16
Infantry Bn (Para)	- 2 (In role)
Infantry Bn (NI)	- 6 (Resident in Ulster)
Infantry Bn (Gurkha)	- 2
Infantry Bn (TA)	- 32
Fire Support Bn (TA)	- 4

Armoured Infantry Battalion
(Commander - Lt Colonel)

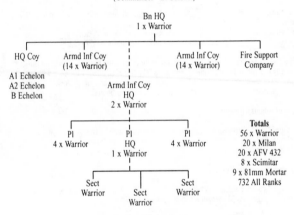

Bn HQ
1 x Warrior

HQ Coy — Armd Inf Coy (14 x Warrior) — Armd Inf Coy (14 x Warrior) — Fire Support Company

A1 Echelon
A2 Echelon
B Echelon

Armd Inf Coy
HQ
2 x Warrior

Pl
4 x Warrior

Pl
HQ
1 x Warrior

Pl
4 x Warrior

Sect Warrior — Sect Warrior — Sect Warrior

Totals
56 x Warrior
20 x Milan
20 x AFV 432
8 x Scimitar
9 x 81mm Mortar
732 All Ranks

Armoured Infantry Battalion - Fire Support Company
(Commander - Major)
2 x Warrior

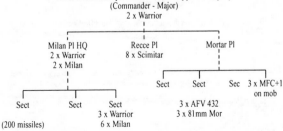

Milan Pl HQ
2 x Warrior
2 x Milan

Recce Pl
8 x Scimitar

Mortar Pl

Sect — Sect — Sect
3 x Warrior
6 x Milan

(200 missiles)

Sect — Sect — Sec   3 x MFC+1
on mob

3 x AFV 432
3 x 81mm Mor

Note: (1) There are 8 x Armoured Infantry Battalions, 6 of which are in Germany with 1 (UK) Armoured Division and the remaining 2 in the UK with 3 (UK) Division. (2) There are plans to replace the AFV 432's on issue to armoured infantry battalions with a new Multi-role Armoured Vehicle (MRAV) by the year 2005. 3) Another 4 Milan firing posts are held by the mobilisation section that is only activated in time of deployment for war.

Mechanised Infantry Battalion
(Commander - Lt Colonel)

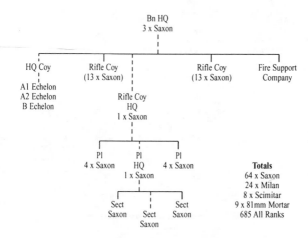

Totals
64 x Saxon
24 x Milan
8 x Scimitar
9 x 81mm Mortar
685 All Ranks

Mechanised Infantry Battalion - Fire Support Company
(Commander - Major)

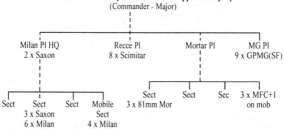

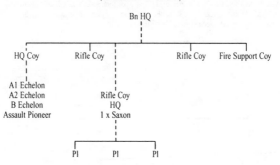

Light Role Infantry Battalion
(Commander - Lt Colonel)

Bn HQ

HQ Coy — Rifle Coy — Rifle Coy — Fire Support Coy

A1 Echelon
A2 Echelon
B Echelon
Assault Pioneer

Rifle Coy
HQ
1 x Saxon

Pl — Pl — Pl

Totals
6 x Milan
9 x 81mm Mortars
625 All Ranks

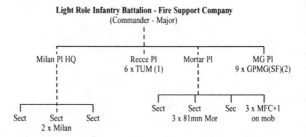

Light Role Infantry Battalion - Fire Support Company
(Commander - Major)

Milan Pl HQ — Recce Pl — Mortar Pl — MG Pl
6 x TUM (1) — 9 x GPMG(SF)(2)

Sect — Sect — Sect
2 x Milan

Sect — Sect — Sec — 3 x MFC+1
3 x 81mm Mor — on mob

Notes:
(1) TUM is the abbreviation for Truck Utility-Medium;
(2) General Purpose Machine Guns mounted on tripods with a range of up to 1,800 metres.

Territorial Army Infantry Battalion

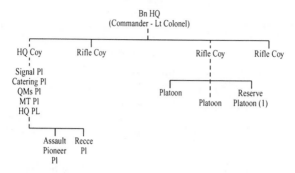

Notes: (1) On mobilisation the reserve platoon would be activated and manned by reservists. (2) TA battalions with a role in support of the ARRC have Milan and Mortar Platoons attached from the TA Fire Support Battalion as necessary. (3) Expect a TA battalion with a National Defence Role to have approximately 550 men on mobilisation and a battalion with a role in support of the ARRC to have approximately 700.

Territorial Army Fire Support Battalion

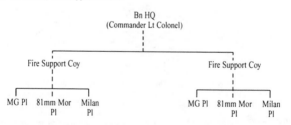

Total strength of this new type of TA battalion will be in the region of approximately 376 personnel. The following TA battalions are being converted to this new role:

       3rd Bn The Prince of Wales's Own Regiment of Yorkshire
       3rd Bn The Cheshire Regiment
       5th Bn The Royal Green Jackets
       51st Highland Volunteers

The TA Fire Support Battalions have now been established and are operational within the Order of Battle.

Platoon Organisation

The basic building bricks of the Infantry Battalion are the platoon and the section. Under normal circumstances expect a British infantry platoon to resemble the organisation in the following diagram:

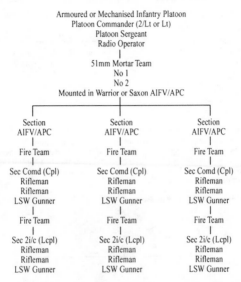

Armoured or Mechanised Infantry Platoon
Platoon Commander (2/Lt or Lt)
Platoon Sergeant
Radio Operator

51mm Mortar Team
No 1
No 2
Mounted in Warrior or Saxon AIFV/APC

Section AIFV/APC	Section AIFV/APC	Section AIFV/APC
Fire Team	Fire Team	Fire Team
Sec Comd (Cpl)	Sec Comd (Cpl)	Sec Comd (Cpl)
Rifleman	Rifleman	Rifleman
Rifleman	Rifleman	Rifleman
LSW Gunner	LSW Gunner	LSW Gunner
Fire Team	Fire Team	Fire Team
Sec 2i/c (Lcpl)	Sec 2i/c (Lcpl)	Sec 2i/c (Lcpl)
Rifleman	Rifleman	Rifleman
Rifleman	Rifleman	Rifleman
LSW Gunner	LSW Gunner	LSW Gunner

Notes: (1) The platoon could be reinforced by a two man team armed with the GPMG in the Sustained Fire (SF) Role. In most regular battalions the GPMG SF gunners are concentrated in the Fire Support Company. (2) The whole platoon with the exception of the LSW (Light Support Weapon) gunners are armed with IW - SA80 (Individual Weapon). (3) The APC could be either Warrior or Saxon and possibly AFV 432. (4) Platoons in armoured or mechanised infantry battalions are armed with the LAW 80 for anti-tank operations. The LAW 80 is issued to other types of infantry battalion when a tank threat exists. (5) During 1996 the riflemen and commanders in each section have been issued with a new rifle grenade sight which can be attached to the SA80. In combat each SA80 user is also issued with two rifle grenades.

The Royal Irish Regiment

The Royal Irish Regiment was formed in July 1992 following the merger of the Ulster Defence Regiment and the Royal Irish Rangers. The Royal Irish Regiment is comprised of 1 x General Service, 1 x TA and 6 x Home Service Battalions.

The soldiers of the General Service Battalion (1 Royal Irish) operate as does any other unit of the Army and in early 1997 the battalion was stationed at Catterick in North Yorkshire. The Home Service battalions serve only in Northern Ireland except for occasional training overseas and include both full time and part time soldiers.

Royal Irish Regiment (Home Service) Strength (1 April 196)

Males	2,702	(Full Time)
Females	312	(Ful Time)
Males	1,819	(Part Time)
Females	303	(Part Time)
	Total 5,136	

General Service	-	1 R Irish
Home Service	-	3 R Irish (Co Down & Co Armagh)
		4 R Irish (Co Fermanagh & Co Tyrone)
		5 R Irish (Co Londonderry)
		7 R Irish (City of Belfast)
		8 R Irish (Co Tyrone)
		9 R Irish (Co Antrim)
		4/5th Rangers (V)

The Special Air Service

The SAS (Special Air Service) can be considered as part of the Infantry and the single regular battalion is designed for special operations. SAS soldiers are selected from other branches of the Army after exhaustive selection tests. There are two regiments of TA SAS.

AFV 432

(Aprox 1,600 in service). Crew 2 (Commander and Driver): Weight loaded 15, 280kg: Length 5.25m: Width 2.8m: Height 2.28m: Ground Pressure 0.78kg km squared: Armament 1 x 7.62 Machine Gun; 2 x 3 barrel smoke dischargers: Engine Rolls Royce K60 No.4 Mark 1-4: Engine Power 240bhp: Fuel Capacity 454 litres: Max Road Speed 52kph: Road Range 580km: Vertical Obstacle 0.9m: Trench Crossing 2.05m: Gradient 60 degrees: Carries up to 10 men : Armour 12.7mm max.

In the medium term the AFV 432 (Trojan) will continue to provide the majority of the British Army's armoured vehicle fleet and it will be some considerable time before all the vehicles in service are replaced. First produced in 1962 and following a development line going back to

WWII, the AFV 432 has been produced in 4 marks, capable of fulfilling about 14 different roles. The most important of these roles are, Command Post APC, 81mm Mor Carrier, Wombat Carrier, Ambulance, Artillery Observation Post, Field Artillery Computing Euipment (FACE) Carrier, Minelayer, Cymbeline Radar Carrier and basic Infantry Carrier.

The vehicle is NBC proof and when necessary can be converted for swimming when it has a water speed of 6kph. Properly maintained it is a rugged and reliable vehicle with a good cross country performance. The most serious drawback is the lack of vision ports for the crew and their subsequent disorientation after dismounting.

The TROJAN (432) is to be replaced possibly as early as 2005 by an infantry variant of a proposed Multi Role Armoured Vehicle (MRAV). This vehicle is a concept vehicle which has yet to reach the drawing board. There are strong reasons to suggest it should be a turretless Warrior but extensive operational analysis and cost comparison exercises will determine whether this will eventually be a completely new vehicle. (For non-infantry roles further back in the battle zone MRAV may be a wheeled version).

MCV - 80 Fv 510 (Warrior)

(789 in Service). Weight loaded 24,500kg: length 6.34m: Height to turret top 2.78m: Width 3.0m: Ground Clearance 0.5m: Max Road Speed 75kph: Road Range 500km: Engine Rolls Royce CV8 diesel: orsepower 550hp: Crew 2 (carries 8 infantry soldiers): Armament L21 30mm Rarden Cannon: Coaxial EX-34 7.62mm Hughes Helicopter Chain Gun: Smoke Dischargers Royal Ordnance Visual and Infra Red Screening Smoke (VIRSS).

Warrior is an armoured infantry fighting vehicle (AIFV) that replaced the AFV 432 in the armoured infantry battalions. Previous plans were for a total build of 1,048 units of which we believe some 600+ had been delivered at the beginning of 1993 with deliveries completed by early 1995.

However, the apparent reduction in the armoured threat forced the UK MOD to look again at the total order and in early 1993 it was announced that the total buy had been reduced to 789 units. Of this total the vast majority had been delivered by early 1995 and the vehicle is in service with 2 armoured infantry battalions in the UK (with 3 (UK) Div) and 6 armoured infantry battalions in Germany (with 1 (UK) Armd Div).

Warrior armed with the 30mm Rarden cannon gives the crew a good chance of destroying enemy APC's at ranges of up to 1,500m and the vehicle carries an infantry section of eight men.

The vehicle is NBC proof, and a full range of night vision equipment is included as standard. The basic Warrior is part of a family of vehicles which includes a mortar carrier, a mechanised recovery vehicle, an engineer combat version and an artillery command vehicle to name but a few. Examination of the contract details reveal that each vehicle will cost approximately £550,000.

The vehicle has seen successful operational service in the Gulf (1991) and with the British contingent serving with the UN in Bosnia. The vehicle has proven protection against mines, and there is dramatic BBC TV footage of a Warrior running over a Serbian anti tank mine with little or no serious damage to the vehicle.

The Kuwait MOD has signed a contract for the purchase of warrior vehicles some of which are Recce vehicles armed with a 90mm Cockerill gun. Industry sources suggest that the Kuwait contract is for 230 vehicles.

The process to update Warrior to hold its place on the future battlefield up to the year 2015 is under way and a Mid Life Improvement (MLI) programme is underway which may result in a different cannon, uprated armour protection and sensors with active decoys or smoke to defeat incoming anti-armour missiles.

AFV 103 Spartan

(400 in service). Crew 3: Weight 8,172kg: Length 5.12m: Height 2.26m: Width 2.26m: Ground Clearance 0.35m: Max Road Speed 80kph: Road Range 483kms: Engine Jaguar J60 No.1 Mark 100B: Engine Power 190bhp: Fuel Capacity 386 litres: Ammunition Carried 3,000 rounds of 7.62mm: Armament 1 x 7.62 Machine Gun.

Spartan is the APC of the Combat Vehicle Reconnaissance Tracked (CVRT) series of vehicles, which includes Fv 101 Scorpion, Fv 102 Striker, Fv 104 Samaritan, Fv 105 Sultan, Fv 106 Sampson and Fv 107 Scimitar. Spartan is a very small APC that can only carry 4 men in addition to the crew of 3. It is therefore used to carry small specialised groups such as the reconnaissance teams, air defence sections, mortar fire controllers and ambush parties.

Samaritan, Sultan and Sampson are also APC type vehicles; Samaritan is the CVRT ambulance vehicle, Sultan is the armoured command vehicle and Sampson is an armoured recovery vehicle.

Spartan, like FV 432 is likely to be replaced by the future Multi Role Armoured Vehicle (MRAV) by the year 2005. In some cases Spartan may be replaced by another future concept vehicle, the Future Liaison Vehicle (FLV).

Spartan is in service with the following nations: Belgium - 266: Oman - 6: Philippines - 7.

AT - 105 Saxon

(655 in service) Weight 10, 670kg: Length 5.16m: Width 2.48m: Height 2.63m: Ground Clearance (axles) 0.33m: Max Road Speed 96kph: Max Road Range 510km: Fuel Capacity 160 litres: Fording 1.12m: Gradient 60 degrees: Engine Bedford 600 6-cylinder diesel developing 164bhp at 2,800rpm: Armour proof against 7.62 rounds fired at point blank range: Crew 2 + 10 max.

The Saxon is manufactured by GKN Defence and the first units for the British Army were delivered in late 1983. The vehicle, which can be best described as a battlefield taxi is designed around truck parts and does not require the enormous maintenance of track and running gear normally associated with APC/ AIFVs. Capable of travelling across very rough terrain and fording over 3' of water, the Saxon is a welcome addition to the inventory of infantry units in UKLF providing much needed battlefield mobility. The vehicle is fitted with a 7.62mm Machine Gun for LLAD.

Each vehicle costs over £100,000 at 1984 prices and they are on issue to 4 mechanised infantry battalions assigned to 3 (UK) Division. The vehicle has been used very successfully by British mechanised battalions serving with the UN in Bosnia. During 1993 the British Army took delivery of the Saxon patrol vehicle for service in Northern Ireland. This new vehicle has a Cummins BT 5.1 engine instead of the Beford 6 cylinder installed on the APC version and other enhancements for internal security operations such as roof mounted searchlights, improved armour, a barricade removal device and an anti-wire device.

Saxon Patrol comes in two versions, troop carrier and ambulance. The troop carrier carries ten men and the ambulance 2 stretcher cases. Industry sources suggest that this latest contract was for 137 vehicles at a cost of some £20 million resulting in a unit cost per vehicle of approximately £145,000.

Some vehicles in the Saxon Battalion are likely to be replaced by the future Multi Role Armoured Vehicle (MRAV) but these do not currently include the Saxon itself.

Saxon is in service with the following overseas customers: Bahrain - 10: Brunei - 24: Hong Kong - 6: Malaysia - 40: Oman - 15.

Fv 18061 Shorland

Weight loaded 3,360kg: Length 4.59m: Height 2.28m: Weight 1.77m: Max Road Speed 88kph: Engine Rover 6-cylinder: Fuel Capacity of 64 litres: Armament 30 Browning or 7.62 machine guns.

Based on the Land Rover chassis, Short Brothers of Belfast produced a lightly armoured vehicle for patrolling in Ulster which is in service with the Royal Ulster Constabulary, and the Royal Irish Regiment.

Milan 2

Missile - Max Range 2,000m; Mix Range 25m; Length 918mm; Weight 6.73Kg; Diameter 125mm; Wing Span 267mm; Rate of Fire 3-4rpm; Warhead Weight 2.70kg; Diameter 115mm; Explosive Content 1.79kg; Firing Post- Weight 16.4kg; Length 900mm; Height 650mm; Width 420mm; Armour Penetration 352mm; Time of Flight to Max Range 12.5 secs; Missile Speed 720kph; Guidance Semi-Automatic command to line of sight by means of wires.

Milan is a second generation anti-tank weapon, the result of a joint development project between France and West Germany with British Milan launchers and missiles built under licence in the UK by British Aerospace Dynamics. We believe that the cost of a Milan missile is currently in the region of £9,000 and that to date the UK MOD has purchased over 50,000 missiles.

The Milan comes in two main components which are the launcher and the missile, it then being a simple matter to clip both items together and prepare the system for use. On firing the operator has only to keep his aiming mark on the target and the SACLOS guidance system will do the rest.

Milan was the first of a series of infantry anti-tank weapons that seriously started to challenge the supremacy of the main battle tank on the battlefield. During fighting in Chad in 1987 it appears that 12 Chadian Milan posts mounted on Toyota Light Trucks were able to account for over 60 Libyan T-55's and T-62's. Reports from other conflicts suggest similar results.

Milan is on issue throughout the British Army and an armoured infantry battalion could be expected to be equipped with 24 firing posts and 200 missiles. In the longer term we expect to see Milan replaced by Trigat MR in the latter part of the decade. Milan is in service with 36 nations world-wide and it is believed that about 800 firing posts are in current service with the British Army.

Trigat MR

Range 2000m: Missile Weight 16kg: Firing Post Weight 20kg.

Trigat MR (Medium Range) is a manportable or vehicle borne, third generation anti-tank missile system designed to replace Milan in service with the British Army. Trigat MR is a medium range missile (2000m) with SACLOS beam riding guidance. Launch will be low velocity, with thrust vectoring keeping the missile airborne as the aerodynamic surfaces come into effect.

71

The missile is the result of a European collaborative project with the three main partners being France, Germany and the UK. The manufacturer is Euromissile Dynamics Group (EDMG). Current predictions are that the missiles may cost as much as £25,000 each by the time that the system is accepted into service. The programme is however subject to some delay and MR Trigat may not enter service until as late as 2005.

The longer range version LR Trigat with an anti-tank battle range out to 4000m remains an unfunded aspiration.

LAW 80

Effective Range Up to 500m: Armour Penetration Up to 650mm: Impact Sensor - Scrub and Foliage Proof: Launcher Length (Firing Mode) 1.5m: Launcher Length (Carrying Mode) 1m: Carrying Weight 10kg: Projectile Diameter 94mm: Temperature Range -46 to +65 degrees C: Rear Danger Area 20m.

LAW 80 has replaced the 84mm Carl Gustav and the US 66mm in service with the British Army, and infantry units in armoured and mechanised battalions are equipped down to section level with this weapon. The latest materials and explosives technology have been utilised in this one-man portable weapon which is capable of destroying main battle tanks at ranges of up to 500m. Outstanding accuracy against both static and moving targets is achieved by the use of a built-in semi-automatic spotting rifle which reduces aiming errors prior to firing the main projectile. This feature roughly doubles the first-shot kill probability and the shaped charge warhead penetrates armour in excess of 650mm. In addition to the low light performance of the built-in sight, full night capability is available using a night sight.

Hunting Engineering has also developed a range of systems to fire the weapon remotely.

Each system utilises a standard LAW 80 with identical tripod and firing unit. ADDERMINE - is suitable as an off-route mine and is fired when a trip or break wire is disturbed. ADDERMINE/ARGES- is a fully autonomous off-route mine system. The programmable sensor package is capable of selecting a particular target before firing. ADDERLAZE - provides the remote capability to engage single or multiple targets at ranges of up to 2kms by the use of a coded laser pulse to fire the weapon.

A replacement has been planned for Law 80 entitled NLAW. This weapon is intended to embody many of the features of Law 80 but have an increased range out to 600 m. There is also a possibility that the weapon will have an inbuilt bunker busting capability. There is a possible in service date of 2004.

66mm HEAT

Maximum Range 300m: Armour Penetration up to 300mm: Weight 2.37kg: Length 0.89 (open), 0.65m (closed) : Calibre 66mm.

The 66mm is the a US designed, hand held, throwaway anti-tank weapon that has been replaced by the LAW 80. Small and light it is easily carried by an infantryman. However, there is doubt as to its ability to destroy the latest MBTs. Some examples of this weapon could continue to be seen for some time and it remains an extremely useful weapon for patrol type tasks.

81mm L16 Mortar

(500 in service) Max Range HE 5,650m: Elevation 45 degrees to 80 degrees: Muzzle Velocity 255m/s: Length of barrel 1280mm: Weight of barrel 12.7kg: Weight of base plate 11.6kg: In action Weight 35.3kg: Bomb Weight HE L3682 4.2kg: Rate of Fire 15rpm: Calibre 81mm.

The 81mm Mortar is on issue to all infantry battalions (with the exception of National Defence TA battalions), with each battalion having a mortar platoon with 3 or 4 sections; and each section deploying 2 mortars. These mortars are the battalions organic fire support and can be used to put a very heavy weight of fire down on an objective in an extremely short period. Mortar fire is particularly lethal to infantry in the open and in addition is very useful for neutralising dug in strongpoints or forcing armour to close down.

The fire of each mortar section is controlled by the MFC (Mortar Fire Controller) who is usually an NCO and generally positioned well forward with the troops being supported. Most MFCs will find themselves either very close to or co-located with a Combat Team commander. The MFC informs the base plate (mortar position) by radio of the location of the target and then corrects the fall of the bombs, directing them onto the target.

Mortar fire can be used to suppress enemy positions until assaulting troops arrive within 200-300m of the position. The mortar fire then lifts onto enemy counter attack and supporting positions while the assault goes in. The 81mm Mortar can also assist with smoke and illuminating rounds. The mortar is carried in an AFV432 or a Land Rover and if necessary can be carried in two man portable 11.35kg loads and one 12.28kg load. In the past, infantry companies have carried one 81mm round per man when operating in areas such as Borneo where wheeled or tracked transport was not available.

With a strong post Gulf War demand for longer range from the 81 mm Mortar a Mortar MidLife Improvement (MLI) programme is under way. The intention is to increase the performance of the barrel, with a minimum increase in weight by the year 2000. By 2005 there should be a new digitised fire control system incorporating a global positioning system or GPS and at an even later date a completely new range of ammunition.

51mm Light Mortar

(2093 in service) Range 750m: Bomb Weight 800gms (illum), 900gms (smk), 920gms (HE): Rapid Rate of Fire 8rpm: Length of barrel 750mm: Weight Complete 6.275kg: Calibre 51.25mm

The 51mm Light Mortar is a weapon that can be carried and fired by one man, and is found in the HQ of an infantry platoon. The mortar is used to fire smoke, illuminating and HE rounds out to a range of approximately 750m; a short range insert device enables the weapon to be used in close quarter battle situations with some accuracy. The 51mm Light Mortar has replaced the older 1940s 2" mortar.

5.56mm Individual Weapon (IW) (SA 80)

Effective Range 400m: Muzzle Velocity 940m/s: Rate of Fire from 610-775rpm: Weight 4.98kg (with 30 round magazine): Length Overall 785mm: Barrel Length 518mm: Trigger Pull 3.12-4.5kg:

Designed to fire the standard NATO 5.56mm x 45mm round the SA 80 is fitted with an X4 telescopic (SUSAT) sight as standard. The total buy for SA 80 was for 332,092 weapons. Issues of the weapon are believed to have been made as follows:

Royal Navy	7,864
Royal Marines	8,350
Royal Air Force	42,221
MOD Police	1,878
Army	271,779

At 1991/92 prices the total cost of the SA80 Contract was in the order of £384.16 million. By late 1994 some 10,000 SA 80 Night Sights and 3rd Generation Image Intensifier Tubes had been delivered, almost completing the contract.

Prior to the entry of the weapon into general service during 1983, the Infantry Trials and Development Unit (ITDU) at Warminster in Wiltshire conducted comparative tests on both the SA80 and the SLR using the old SLR APWT (Annual Personal Weapons Test) for both weapons. The results were as follows:

Results	SLR	SA80 with SUSAT
Passes	72%	100%
Marksmanship Standard	17%	51%
Average Score	53	60

Note: The highest possible score was 70; the pass mark 49 and the marksmanship standard was 60 out of a possible 70. The APWT has since been amended to take into account the greater accuracy of the SA 80.

The weapon has had a mixed press and much has been made of the 32 modifications that have been made to the SA80 since 1983. In addition, modifications have recently had to be made to enable the weapon to be more reliable when firing 5.56 ammunition supplied by other NATO countries. Although there are many critics outside of the services, in the main the serving soldiers that we have spoken to have praised the weapon, and those that have had experience on both the SLR and SA80 are unstinting in their praise for the newer system.

The bottom line is probably that the SA80 is a highly accurate weapon and one that is more than sound when properly maintained. It's accuracy places it into a different generation from earlier weapons and it needs to be treated with respect for its higher technology. Our own enquiries suggest that it compares favourably with anything else available on the current world market.

The weapon capability has also been extended by the introduction into service of a bullet catcher rifle grenade used in conjunction with a sight fitting issued to individual riflemen and section commanders. Once pulled down over the barrel of the SA80 the grenade is launched by firing a bullet into it which projects it accurately up to 150 m and provides an area suppression capability out to 300 m.

5.56mm Light Support Weapon (LSW)

Range 1,000m: Muzzle Velocity 970m/s: Length 900mm: Barrel Length 646mm: Weight Loaded with 30 round magazine 6.58kg: Rate of Fire 610-775rpm.

The LSW has been developed to replace the GPMG in the light role and about 80% of the parts are interchangeable with the 5.56 IW (SA 80). A great advantage for the infantryman is the ability of both weapons to take the same magazines. A rifle section will have two x 4 man fire teams and each fire team 1 x LSW.

The LSW is currently experiencing some difficulty in firing 5.56 ammunition supplied by other NATO countries. This problem is under review.

An Image Intensifier night sight, the CWS, has been produced for LSW which gives excellent night vision out to 400 m.

7.62mm General Purpose Machine Gun (GPMG)

Range 800 (Light Role), 1,800m (Sustained Fire Role): Muzzle Velocity 538m/s: Length 1.23m: Weight loaded 13.85kg (gun + 50 rounds); Belt Fed: Rate of Fire up to 750rpm: Rate of Fire Light Role 100rpm: Rate of Fire Sustained Fire Role 200rpm.

An infantry machine gun which has been in service since the early 1960s, the GPMG can be used in the light role fired from a bipod or can be fitted to a tripod for use in the sustained fire role. The gun is also found pintle mounted on many armoured vehicles. Used on a tripod the gun is effective out to 1,800m although it is difficult to spot strike at this range because the tracer rounds in the ammunition belt burns out at 1,100m. The GPMG has been replaced in the light role by the 5.56mm Light Support Weapon (LSW). The LSW weighs approximately half as much as the GPMG. Machine Gun platoons in infantry battalions remain equipped with the GPMG in the sustained fire role.

A new heavy machine gun, is planned to come into service by the year 2004. In the meantime the GPMG performance is being enhanced by the issue of a Maxi Kite night image intensification sight giving excellent visibility out to 600m.

CHAPTER 6 - ARTILLERY

"Of the 100 guns in my brigade 87 survived the air attacks while only 17 survived the artillery bombardment."

Captured Iraqi Artillery Brigadier Gulf War 1991.

"I confess that I was relieved when it came to an end. I am not saying that I felt sorry for the enemy, but I was quite certain that half an hour of the bombardment would be enough to render him nearly helpless when we advanced."

Brigadier Patrick Cordingley, Commander 7 Armd Bde Gulf War 1991.

The Royal Regiment of Artillery (RA)

The RA provides the battlefield fire support and air defence for the British Army in the field. Its various regiments are equipped for conventional fire support using field guns, for area and point air defence using air defence missiles and for specialised artillery locating tasks. By September 1990 the first Regiment equipped with the Multiple Launch Rocket System (MLRS) had taken its place in the Order of Battle and these weapons were used with great effect during the war in the Gulf. In October 1993 1st Royal Horse Artillery became the first regiment to be equipped with the AS 90 self propelled howitzer.

At the beginning of 1997 the RA, one of the larger organisations in the British Army with 17 Regiments included in its regular Order of Battle, has the following structure in both the UK and Germany (ARRC).

	UK	Germany
Field Regiments (AS 90 SP Guns)	2	3
Field Regiments (Light Gun)	3(1)	-
Depth Fire Regiments (MLRS)	3	-
Air Defence Regiments (Rapier)	2	-
Air Defence Regiment (Javelin)	1	-
Air Defence Regiment (HVM)	-	1
Training Regiment	1	-
The Kings Troop (Ceremonial)	1	-

Note:

(1) Of these 3 Regiments one is a Commando Regiment (29 Cdo Regt) and another is a Parachute Regiment (7 PARA RHA), both of these regiments are equipped with the Light Gun as is the UK Force Artillery Regiment (AMF).

(2) Although the artillery is organised into Regiments, much of a Gunner's loyalty is directed towards the battery in which they serve. A Regiment will generally have three or four gun batteries under command.

The Royal Horse Artillery (RHA) is also part of the Royal Regiment of Artillery and its three regiments have been included in the totals above. There is considerable cross posting from the RA to the RHA, and some consider service with the RHA to be a career advancement.

Artillery recruits spend the first period of recruit training (Phase 1 Training, Common Military

Syllabus) at the Army Training Regiment - Pirbright. Artillery training (Phase 2) is carried out at the Royal School of Artillery at Larkhill in Wiltshire. After Phase 2 training officers and gunners will be posted to RA units world-wide, but soldiers will return to the RSA for frequent career and (Phase 3) employment courses.

The current (1 Jan 1997) permanent locations of the Regular Regiments of the Royal Artillery are as follows:

United Kingdom

1 Regiment RHA	Tidworth	155mm AS 90
3 Regiment RHA	Topcliffe	155mm AS 90
5 Regiment RA	Catterick	MLRS & Special Operations
7 Parachute Regiment RHA	Aldershot	105mm Lt Gun Javelin
14 Regiment RA	Larkhill	All Equipments
19 Regiment RA	Colchester	105mm Lt Gun
Regiment RA	Kirton-in-Lindsey	Rapier and Javelin
29 Commando Regiment RA*	Plymouth	105mm Light Gun
47 Regiment RA	Thorney Island	Javelin
32 Regiment RA	Larkhill	MLRS & Locating Eqpt
16 Regiment RA	Woolwich	Rapier
39 Regiment RA	Harlow Hill	MLRS
The Kings Troop RHA	London	13 Pounders (Ceremonial)

Note: The Regimental HQ of 29 Commando Regiment with one battery is at Plymouth. The other two batteries are at Arbroath and Poole.

Germany

4 Regiment RA	Osnabruck	155mm AS 90
12 Regiment RA	Dortmund	HVM
26 Regiment RA	Gutersloh	155mm AS 90
40 Regiment RA	Hohne	155mm AS 90

The diverse equipment available to artillery and the computerised locating and fire control systems now coming into service, combined with "intelligent" munitions and long range weapon platforms are creating another revolution in tactical thinking. In the longer term these developments may have the same effect on land warfare as the emergence of the tank.

A new generation of Rocket Launchers (MLRS) and Self Propelled Field Guns (AS 90), with very long ranges and ordnance with devastating terminal effect are now part of the battlefield. These weapons, fearsome though they may be, are all the more destructive when linked to modern target location systems. These locating systems, such as small, fast and highly manoeuvrable remotely piloted vehicles are capable of flying out over enemy territory, sending back real time up to the minute pictures (including thermal imagery) of the target area and assisting observers in directing the rounds onto the target.

Artillery has always been a cost effective way of destroying or neutralising targets. When the cost of a battery of guns, (approx £10 million) is compared with the cost of a close air support aircraft, (£20 million) and the cost of training each pilot, (£3 million +) the way ahead for governments with less and less to spend on defence is clear.

Air Defence is a vital part of the role of the Royal Artillery and updates to the Rapier system continue, and batteries being upgraded to Field Standard B2 and Field Standard C. During 1994 a Starstreak HVM Regiment became operational in the UK. In addition, the air defences will be enhanced by the Air Defence Alerting Device for Javelin and Starstreak, and the Air Defence Command, Control and Information System entered service during late 1994.

The Royal Artillery provides the modern British armoured formation with a protective covering. The air defence covers the immediate airspace above and around the formation, with the field artillery reaching out to approximately 30kms in front and across the flanks of the formation. An armoured formation that moves out of this protective covering is open to immediate destruction by an intelligent enemy.

Divisional Artillery Group (DAG)

An armoured or mechanised division has it own artillery under command. This artillery usually consists of 3 Close Support Regiments, with a number of units detached from the Corps Artillery and could include TA reinforcements from the UK. In war the composition of the DAG will vary from division to division according to the task.

Armoured Divisional Artillery Group (DAG)

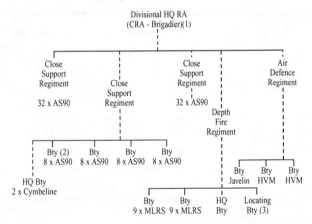

Notes:
(1) This is a diagram of the artillery support which may typically be available to an Armd Div deployed with the ARRC. Expect each brigade in the division to have one Close Support Regiment with AS 90. Following full scale mobilisation this artillery force could be reinforced by a TA FH70 Regiment with 3 x 6 gun batteries (18 guns in total) and 2 x Cymbeline. Artillery regiments are commanded by a Lieutenant Colonel and a battery is commanded by a Major.
(2) The number of batteries and guns per battery in an AS90 Close Support Regiment has been

finally resolved at 4 batteries of eight guns per battery, to enable the 4 battlegroups in each brigade to be fully supported. Although a battery has eight guns on establishment only six guns will be manned in peacetime.

(3) The locating Battery in the Depth Fire Regiment will have the following configuration:

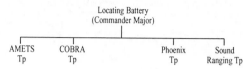

(3) Area Air Defence (AAD) is provided by Rapier and the divisional area could easily be covered by one Rapier Battery.

(4) The staff of an armoured or mechanised division includes a Brigadier of Artillery known as the Commander Royal Artillery (CRA). The CRA acts as the artillery advisor to the Divisional Commander, and could normally assign one of his Close Support Regiments to support each of the Brigades in the division. These regiments would be situated in positions that would allow most of their batteries to fire across the complete divisional front. Therefore, in the very best case, a battlegroup under extreme threat could be supported by the fire of more than 96 guns.

Artillery Fire Support

A square brigade (of two infantry battalions and two armoured regiments) will probably have a Close Support Regiment of 4 Batteries in support, and the CO of this regiment will act as the artillery advisor to the Brigade Commander.

It would be usual to expect that each of the 4 battlegroups in the brigade would have a Battery Commander acting as the artillery advisor to the Battlegroup Commander. Squadron/ Company Groups in the Battlegroup would each be provided with a Forward Observation Officer (FOO), who is responsible for fire planning and directing the fire of the guns onto the target. The FOO and his party travel in armoured vehicles to enable them to keep up with the formation being supported and are generally in contact with:

    (a) The Gun Positions
    (b) The Battery Commander at BGHQ
    (c) The Regimental Fire Direction Centre
    (d) The Company Group being supported.

Having identified the target, the FOO will call for fire from the guns, and he will then adjust the fall of shot to cover the target area. The FOO will be assisted in this task by the use of a Warrior OP vehicle containing the computerised fire control equipment which provides accurate data of the target location.

Given a vehicle with its surveillance and target acquisition suite the FOO can almost instantly obtain the correct grid of the target and without calling for corrections, order 1 round fire for effect.

AS 90

179 in Service: Crew 5: Length 9.07m: Width 3.3m: Height 3.0m overall: Ground Clearance 0.41m: Turret Ring Diameter 2.7m: Armour 17mm: Calibre 155mm: Range (39 cal) 24.7kms (52 cal) 30kms: Recoil Length 780mm: Rate of Fire 3 rounds in 10 secs (burst) 6 rounds per minute (intense) 2 rounds per minute (sustained): Secondary Armament 7.62mm MG: Traverse 6,400 mills: Elevation -89/+1.244 mills: Ammunition Carried 48 x 155mm projectiles and charges (31 turret & 17 hull): Engine Cumminis VTA903T turbo-charged V8 diesel 660hp: Max Speed 53 kph: Gradient 60%: Vertical Obstacle 0.75m: Trench Crossing 2.8m: Fording Depth 1.5m: Road Range 420kms.

AS 90 is manufactured by Vickers Shipbuilding and Engineering (VSEL) at Barrow in Furness and has recently been the subject of an order for 179 guns under a fixed price contract for £300 million. These 179 guns will equip 5 field regiments completely replacing the Abbot and M109 in British service. The first Regiment to receive AS 90 was 1st Regiment Royal Horse Artillery (1 RHA) in October 1993, followed by issues to 3 RHA, 4 Regt, 40 Regt and 26 Regt. Three of these Regiments will be under the command of 1(UK) Armoured Division in Germany and two under the command of 3 (UK) Div in the United Kingdom.

AS 90 is currently equipped with a 39 calibre gun which fires the NATO L15 unassisted projectile out to a range of 24.7kms (RAP range is 30kms). Future production models will have the 52 calibre gun with ranges of 30kms (unassisted) and 40kms (assisted projectile). Indications are that the current in service date for the 52 calibre gun is 1998.

AS 90 has been fitted with an autonomous navigation and gun laying system (AGLS), enabling it to work independently of external sighting references. Central to the system is an inertial dynamic reference unit (DRU) taken from the US Army's MAPS (Modular Azimuth Positioning System). The bulk of the turret electronics are housed in the Turret Control Computer (TCC) which controls the main turret functions, including gunlaying, magazine control, loading systems control, power distribution and testing.

227mm MLRS

62 launchers in service - 54 operational in 3 Regiments): Crew 3: Weight loaded 24,756kg: Weight Unloaded 19,573kg: Length 7.167m: Width 2.97m: Height (stowed) 2.57m: Height (max elevation) 5.92m: Ground Clearance 0.43m: Max Road Speed 64kph: Road Range 480km: Fuel Capacity 617 litres: Fording 1.02m: Vertical Obstacle 0.76m: Engine Cummings VTA-903 turbocharged 8 cylinder diesel developing 500 bhp at 2,300 rpm: Rocket Diameter 227mm:

Rocket Length 3.93m: M77 Bomblet Rocket Weight 302.5kg: AT2 SCATMIN Rocket Weight 254.46kg: M77 Bomblet Range 11.5 -32kms: AT2 SCATMIN Rocket Range 39kms: One round Fire for Effect equals one launcher firing 12 rockets: Ammunition Carried 12 rounds (ready to fire).

The MLRS is based on the US M2 Bradley chassis and the system is self loaded with 2 x rocket pod containers, each containing 6 x rockets. The whole loading sequence is power assisted and loading takes between 20 and 40 minutes. There is no manual procedure.

A single round Fire for Effect (12 rockets) delivers 7728 bomblets or 336 scatterable mines and the coverage achieved is considered sufficient to neutralise a 500m x 500m target or produce a minefield of a similar size. The weapon system is range dependent and therefore more rounds will be required to guarantee the effect as the range to the target increases. Ammunition for the MLRS is carried on the DROPS vehicle which is a Medium Mobility Load Carrier. Each DROPS vehicle with a trailer can carry 8 x Rocket Pod Containers and there are 15 x DROPS vehicles supporting the 9 x M270 Launcher vehicles within each MLRS battery.

The handling of MLRS is almost a military art form and is an excellent example of the dependence of modern artillery on high technology. Getting the best out of the system is more than just parking the tubes and firing in the direction of the enemy. MLRS is the final link in a chain that includes almost everything available on the modern battlefield, from high speed communications, collation of intelligence, logistics and a multitude of high technology artillery skills and drills. Remotely piloted vehicles can be used to acquire targets, real time TV and data links are used to move information from target areas to formation commanders and onward to the firing positions. Helicopters can be used to dump ammunition and in some cases to move firing platforms.

MLRS is deployed as independent launcher units, using shoot-and-scoot techniques. A battery of nine launchers will be given a battery manoeuvre area (BMA), within which are allocated three troop manoeuvre areas (TMA). These TMAs will contain close hides, survey points and reload points. In a typical engagement, a single launcher will be given its fire mission orders using burst data transmission.

An important initial piece of information received is the drive on angle; the crew will drive the launcher out of the hide (usually less than 100m) and align it with this angle. Using the navigation equipment, its location is fed into the ballistic computer which already has the full fire mission details. The launcher is then elevated and fired and the process can take as little as a few minutes to complete.

As soon as possible after firing, the vehicle will leave the firing location and go to a reload point where it will unload the empty rocket pods and pick up a full one; this can be done in less than five minutes. It will then go to a new hide within the TMA via a survey point to check the accuracy of the navigation system (upon which the accuracy of fire is entirely dependent). The whole of this cycle is coordinated centrally, and details of the new hide and reload point are received as part of the fire mission orders. The complete cycle from firing to being in a new hide ready for action might take half an hour.

In a typical day, a battery could move once or twice to a new BMA but this could impose a strain upon the re-supply system unless well planned (bearing in mind the need for the amunition to be in position before the launcher vehicle arrives in a new BMA). The frequent moves are a result of security problems inherent in MLRS's use. In addition to attack by radar-controlled counterbattery fire, its effectiveness as an interdiction weapon makes it a valuable target for special-forces units. Although MLRS will be hidden amongst friendly forces up to 15km behind the FEBA, its firing signature and small crew (three) will force it to move continually to avoid an actual confrontation with enemy troops.

The US Army is currently operating 416 MLRS and by the middle of the decade the French will have 82, the West Germans 206 and the Italians 21.

FH 70 Howitzer

(36 in service) Crew 8: Weight (in firing position) 8,800kg: Length 9.45m: Height 2.56m: Ammunition HE, Anti Tank, Smoke, Illuminating: Maximum Range HE 24kms: Calibre 155mm: Rate of Fire 6 rounds per minute: Shell Weight (HE) 43.5kg: Engine Volkswagen 1,795cc petrol producing 76bhp with a 20km range.

The FH 70 is the result of a NATO collaborative project between Italy, West Germany and the United Kingdom. The first FH 70 were delivered to the British Army in 1978 and there are now 36 guns in service with two TA Regiments (100 and 101 Field Regiments).

The gun is designed to enable NATO forces to use the 155mm round which is capable of disrupting massed armoured formations. The gun is towed into action by the FH 70 Foden, 6 x 6 Tractor and in emergencies, can use a small petrol engine mounted on the gun to move short distances on the battlefield.

With a range of 24kms and a calibre of 155mm, the FH 70 is a considerable improvement on both the Abbot and M109. The gun is in service with West Germany (216), Italy (164), audi Arabia (72), Malaysia (30), Oman (12) and Japan (200).

105mm Light Gun

(72 in service). Crew 6: Weight 1,858kg: Length 8.8m: Width 1.78m: Height 21.3m: Ammunition HE, HEAT, WP, Smoke, Illuminating, Target Marking: Maximum Range (HE) 17.2kms: Anti Tank Range 800m: Muzzle Velocity 709m/s: Shell Weight HE 15.1kg: Rate of Fire 6 rounds per minute.

The Light Gun is in service with the UK Parachute and Commando Field Artillery Regiments as a go-anywhere, airportable weapon which can be carried around the battlefield underslung on a Puma or Chinook. The gun was first delivered to the British Army in 1975 and since that time it has replaced the older 105m Pack Howitzer. A robust, reliable system, the gun proved its worth in the Falklands, where guns were sometimes firing up to 400 rounds per day.

The Light Gun has been extremely successful in the international market with sales to Australia (59), Botswana (6), Brunei (6), Ireland (12), Kenya (40), Malawi (12), Malaysia (20), Morocco (36), New Zealand (34), Oman (39), Switzerland (6), UAE (50), United States (548) and Zimbabwe (12).

Javelin

(382 Fire Units in Service) Length 1.4m: Missile Diameter 76 cm: Missile Weight 11.1 kgs: Max Range 5.5kms: Warhead Weight 2.72 kgs: Max Altitude 3,000 feet: Max Speed Mach 1.7+: Fuse Proximity or Impact: Guidance SACLOS; Mount Man Portable.

Javelin is the British Army's successor to Blowpipe and is in service with one regular regiment and 2 TA regiments in the UK.

47 Regiment RA is the regular regiment equipped with Javelin and supports 3 (UK) Division with batteries supporting brigades as follows:-

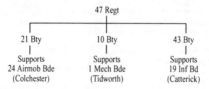

```
                              47 Regt
                                 |
        +------------------------+------------------------+
        |                        |                        |
     21 Bty                   10 Bty                    43 Bty
        |                        |                        |
    Supports                 Supports                 Supports
  24 Airmob Bde            1 Mech Bde               19 Inf Bd
   (Colchester)             (Tidworth)              (Catterick)
```

Javelin is an electronically more sophisticated system than Blowpipe with a greater range and a night sight. The greatest advantage is that it is now SACLOS guided, and all the operator has to do is keep the aiming mark on the target, leaving the guidance system to do the rest.

Javelin is a highly accurate system. Target practice during Javelin testing in 1985 presented the British Army with a problem regarding the numbers of available target drones. So many target drones were being destroyed during training that testing had to be slowed down until the manufacture of target drones caught up.

Javelin is deployed in armoured vehicles (Spartan or AFV 432) or wheeled vehicles to provide point air defence for troops in the forward areas of the battlefield. A Javelin battery normally has 36 launchers.

In time it is possible that Javelin may be mounted on AAC helicopters and a naval version (Sea Javelin) is already available. In the longer term it is envisaged that Javelin will be entirely replaced by Starstreak in British service.

There is already considerable overseas interest in Javelin which is believed to cost about £60,000 per missile at 1989 prices. Sales have already been made to Jordan and South Korea with potential customers believed to be Malaysia, Chile, Oman and Zimbabwe.

Javelin's predecessor Blowpipe, achieved considerable success in the world market and we believe that over 30,000 missiles have been manufactured by 1997, with sales being made to the following - Canada, Chile, Ecuador, Malawi, Nigeria, Oman, Portugal, Qatar, and Thailand. Guerrilla forces in both Angola and Afghanistan are known to have acquired Blowpipe missiles.

Starstreak

(135 Fire Units In Service) Missile Length 1.39m: Missile Diameter 0.27m: Missile Speed Mach 4+: Maximum Range 7 kms: Minimum Range 300m.

Short Brothers of Belfast are the prime contractors for the Starstreak HVM (Hyper Velocity Missile) which continues along the development path of both Blowpipe and Javelin. The system can be shoulder launched using the LML (lightweight multiple launcher) or vehicle borne on the Alvis Stormer APC. The Stormer APC has an eight round launcher and 20 reload missiles can be carried inside the vehicle.

Starstreak which has been designed to counter threats from very high performance low flying aircraft and fast pop-up type strikes by attack helicopters, can easily be retrofitted to existing Blowpipe and Javelin equipment. The missile employs a system of three dart type projectiles which can make multiple hits on the target. Each of these darts has an explosive warhead combined with a chemical and kinetic energy penetrating shell. It is believed that the Starstreak has an SSK (single shot to kill) probability of over 95%.

12 Regiment RA stationed in German is equipped with HVM and supports 1 (UK) Division. This regiment is configured as follows:

12 Regiment RA

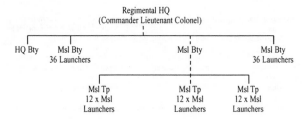

Note: The Regiment has 108 launchers divided amongst the three missile batteries. A launcher detachment is carried in a Stormer armoured vehicle and in each vehicle there are 3 personnel. Inside the vehicle there are eight ready to use missiles with a further 20 stored inside as reloads.

Rapier

(40 fire units in service) Guidance Semi Automatic to Line of Sight (SACLOS): Missile Diameter 13.3 cm: Missile Length 2.35m: Rocket Solid Fuelled: Warhead High Explosive: Launch Weight 42kg: Speed Mach 2+: Ceiling 3,000m: Maximum Range 6,800m: Fire Unit Height 2.13m: Fire Unit Weight 1,227kg: Radar Height (in action) 3.37m: Radar Weight 1,186kg: Optical Tracker Height 1.54m: Optical Tracker Weight 119kg: Generator Weight 243kg: Generator Height 0.91m.

The Rapier system provides area, Low Level Air Defence (LLAD) over the battlefield. It consists of an Optical Tracker, a Fire Unit, a Radar and a Generator. The into-action time of the system is thought to be about 15 minutes and the radar is believed to scan out to 12km. Each fire unit can therefore cover an Air Defence Area (ADA) of about 100 square kms. Having discharged the 4 missiles on a Fire Unit, 2 men are thought to be able to carry out a reload in about 3 minutes.

The Royal Artillery has two regiments equipped with Rapier and both are in the UK. These regiments have 3/4 batteries and each battery 10 fire units. In the Falklands Campaign, Rapier was credited with 14 kills and 6 probables from a total of 24 missiles fired.

In the longer term there will be a further upgrade to Field Standard C (FSC) and that three batteries (31 fire units) of this equipment are on order. The towed system launcher will mount eight missiles (able to fire two simultaneously) which will be manufactured in two warhead versions. One of these warheads will be armour piercing to deal with fixed wing targets, and the other a fragmentation warhead for the engagement of cruise missiles and RPVs. Rapier FSC will have the Darkfire tracker and a tailor made 3-dimensional radar system for target acquisition developed by Plessey. The total cost of the Rapier FSC programme is £1,886 million.

Rapier has now been sold to the armed forces of at least 14 nations. We believe that sales have amounted to over 25,000 missiles, 600 launchers and 350 Blindfire radars.

Sound Ranging

Sound Ranging locates the positions of enemy artillery from the sound of their guns firing. Microphones are positioned on a line extending over a couple of kilometres to approximately 12 kilometres. As each microphone detects the sound of enemy guns firing the information is relayed to a Command Post which computes the location of the enemy battery. Enemy locations are then passed to Artillery Intelligence and counter battery tasks fired as necessary. Sound Ranging can identify an enemy position to within 50 metres at 10 kms

MSTAR

Weight 30 kg: Wavelength J - Band: Range in excess of 20 kms.

MSTAR is a Lightweight Pulse Doppler J - Band All Weather Radar that has replaced the ZB 298 in the detection of helicopters, vehicles and infantry. Powered by a standard army field battery this radar will also assist the artillery observer in detecting the fall of shot. The electroluminescent display that shows dead ground relief and target track history, also has the ability to superimpose a map grid at the 1:50000 scale to ease transfer to military maps. MSTAR can be vehicle borne or broken down into three easily transportable loads for manpacking purposes.

MSTAR has been delivered to the Royal Artillery and will be used by Forward Observation Officers. In time there should be over 100 MAOV (Warrior Mechanised Artillery Observation Vehicles) equipped with MSTAR. MSTAR is believed to cost about £50,000 per unit at 1993 prices, and by the late 1990s we see a requirement for over 250 MSTAR equipments for use throughout the British Army.

COBRA

Cobra is a 3-D Phased Array Radar that is being developed for West Germany, France and the UK with a planned deployment date for the equipment towards the end of the decade. We currently expect between 30 and 40 radars to be ordered with West Germany ordering about 15 systems, France 15 and the UK 10. The current price estimate for a single equipment is in the region of £10 million at 1996 prices. The dominant cost element of the Cobra Radar is the antenna, which probably accounts for about 70% of the unit price. There are believed to be about 20,000 Gallium Arsenide integrated circuits in each antenna.

Until very recently, companies involved in the Cobra project were forbidden to give details of the programme and information is still almost impossible to obtain. What is known is that the equipment will be able to produce the locations of enemy artillery at extremely long ranges, and the radar will be able to cope with saturation type bombardments . In addition there will be a high degree of automated software, with high speed circuitry and secure data transmission to escape detection from enemy electronic countermeasures.

Cobra therefore appears to be an ideal equipment for operation in conjunction with MLRS. However, the inservice date for the equipment was originally the late 1990s and the MoD has recently acknowledged that the programme is approximately 6 years behind schedule and there is probably little chance that it will appear much before 2005. It is believed that when the equipment becomes available the British Army will field three Cobra Troops, each Troop consisting of three radars.

If orders are confirmed, production is expected to peak at 14 radars per year in 1997 and run on until 2001. The British Army is currently looking at an in service date (ISD) of November 1998.

Cymbeline Mortar Locating Radar

(10 in service) Range 20kms: Weight of Radar 390kgs: Frequency I/J Band:

Cymbeline is the mortar locating radar which is currently under the command of the Close Support Regiments in both Germany and the UK. Cymbeline is mounted on an AFV 432.

Cymbeline detects the flight path of a mortar bomb at two points in the trajectory as it passes through the radar beam(s), rapid computing then enables the grid reference of the enemy base plate to be identified and engaged with artillery. An 81 mortar bomb can be detected at a range of about 10 kms while a 120mm bomb is detectable at about 14 kms.

Cymbeline first came into service with the British Army in 1973 and will probably stay in service for some time to come, with the possibility of a further Mark 4 upgrade to the present Mark 3 systems. Cymbeline is deployed with the AS 90 regiments and the TA FH70 Regiments.

In 1994 Cymbeline was deployed by the British Army in support of United Nations operations in the Sarajevo area of the Former Yugoslavia to identify gun and mortar positions around the city. The equipment appears to have been extremely successful in this role and has provided much valuable intelligence for the UN Command Staff. The equipment was used extensively during the late 1995 UN bombardment of Serb artillery positions.

At the beginning of 1997 we believe that over 325 Cymbeline were in service with 18 nations, including Singapore, Norway, Denmark, Finland, Oman, Saudi Arabia, Egypt, Kuwait, Nigeria, South Africa, Malawi, Switzerland and New Zealand.

Phoenix

Phoenix is an all weather, day or night, real time surveillance system which consists of a variety of elements. It was developed under a contract initially awarded in 1985. The twin boom UAV (unmanned air vehicle) provides surveillance through its surveillance pod, the imagery from which is datalinked via a ground data terminal (GDT) to a ground control station (GCS). This controls the overall Phoenix mission and is used to distribute the UAV provided intelligence direct to artillery forces, to command level, or to a Phoenix troop command post (TCP). The principle method of communication from the GCS to artillery on the ground is via the battlefield artillery engagement system (BATES).

Powered by a 19kW (25hp) Target Technology 342 two stroke flat twin engine, the Phoenix air vehicle (with a centrally mounted fuel tank) is almost entirely manufactured from composites such as Kevlar, glass fibre, carbon reinforced plastics and Nomex honeycomb. The principal subcontractor is Flight Refueling of Christchurch in Dorset.

The modular design UAV can be launched within one hour of reaching a launch site and a second UAV can be dispatched within 8 minutes from the same launcher. The wing span is 5.5m and the maximum launch weight 175kgs. The manufacture, GEC states that Flight endurance is in excess of 4 hours, radius of action 50kms and the maximum altitude 2,700m (9,000 feet).

A flight section consists of a launch and recovery detachment and a ground control detachment. The launch and recovery detachment consists of three vehicles; the launch support vehicle, with several UAVs and mission pods in separate battlefield containers, plus operational replacement spares and fuel; the launch vehicle, which features a pallet-mounted lifting crane,the hydraulic catapult and launch ramp, a pre-launch detonator device, built-in test equipment, and the Land Rover recovery vehicle which is fitted with cradles for the air vehicle and mission pod. The ground-control detachment consists of two vehicles, the ground control station and the Land Rover towed ground data terminal.

The British Army has ordered three troops of Phoenix (approx 50 UAV) and believe that a troop will probably have about 10 - 15 UAV with associated ground support equipment. Of these three Phoenix troops, two will be operational and the third a reserve/training unit. The total cost of the programme is £227 million.

The Phoenix programme has been delayed due to technical difficulties and the latest inservice date is now believed to be October 1997.

AMETS

An AMETS troop is responsible for providing the staff with up-to-date information regarding local weather conditions for use by artillery and NBC operators. AMETS troops are generally 20 strong, and the troop is usually part of a larger Locating Battery that has two other troops, one of which is dedicated to Sound Ranging and the other to unmanned surveillance aircraft operations.

With the extreme range of modern artillery and battlefield missiles, very precise calculations regarding wind and density are needed to ensure that the target is accurately engaged.

AMETS units can provide this information by releasing hydrogen filled balloons at hourly intervals recording important information on weather conditions at various levels of the atmosphere. The AMETS Troop travels in 4 ton box body vehicles. AMETS will in due course be replaced by BMETS.

Air Defence Alerting System (ADAD)

An infra-red thermal imaging search and track system that is used by air defence units to detect hostile aircraft and helicopter targets and directs weapon systems into the target area. The air defence missile operators can be alerted to up to four targets in a priority order. The passive system which is built by Thorn EMI has an all weather, day and night capability.

CHAPTER 7 - ARMY AVIATION

> *"Float like a butterfly - sting like a bee".*
>
> Muhammad Ali.

> *"Airpower is like poker. A second best hand is like none at all - it will cost you dough and win you nothing at all".*
>
> General George C Kenney
> USAF.

The Army obtains its aviation support from two agencies. The first is the Army Air Corps (AAC), which is an Army organisation with 5 separate regiments and a number of independent squadrons. The AAC also provides support for Northern Ireland on a mixed resident and roulement basis and the two squadrons concerned are sometimes referred to as the sixth AAC Regiment, although the units would disperse on mobilisation and have no regimental title.

By late 1996 and following the Options for Change restructuring AAC regimental locations were as follows:

1 Regiment	-	Germany	(651, 652 & 661 Sqns)
3 Regiment	-	Wattisham	(653, 662 & 663 Sqns)
4 Regiment	-	Wattisham	(654,659 & 669 Sqns)
5 Regiment	-	Aldergrove	(655 & 665 Sqns)
7 Regiment	-	Netheravon	(658 & 666(V) Sqns)
9 Regiment	-	Dishforth	(656, 657 & 664 Sqns)

The HQ of 2 (Trg) Regiment is at Middle Wallop and there are TA Flights at Netheravon, Turnhouse and Shawbury.

In addition to the Regiments in the UK and Germany there are small flights in Cyprus, Bruggen (Germany), Brunei, Suffield (Canada) and the Falklands Islands.

The AAC Centre at Middle Wallop in Hampshire acts as a focal point for all Army Aviation, and it is here that the majority of training for pilots and aircrew is carried out. From Mid 1997 elementary flying training for all three services will be carried out at RAF Shawbury in Shropshire.

Although the AAC operates some fixed wing aircraft for training, liaison flying and radar duties, the main effort goes into providing helicopter support for the ground forces. About 350 AAC helicopters are used for anti-tank operations, artillery fire control, reconnaissance, liaison flying and a limited troop lift.

Attack Helicopters

Army aviation is heavily involved in the battlefield revolution that was mentioned earlier in this publication. With the ability to move ground forces around the battlefield at speeds of up to 200kph and the proven ability of anti-tank helicopters to defeat tanks at 5,000m+, the helicopter has approached the point where it could be claimed to be one of the most important equipments on the battlefield. All of the credible military nations have expressed their belief in the importance of the armed helicopter, and the United States leads the way with over 1,400 armed helicopters of which over 700 are AH64 attack types. Many analysts believe that the armed helicopter has a superiority over the tank in the region of 20:1 and recent West German operational analysis figures suggest that this superiority may be even higher.

During the 1991 Gulf War the US Army deployed 288 x AH-64 Apache in 15 Army Aviation battalions. The US Army claim that these aircraft destroyed 120 x APCs, 500 x MBT, 120 x Artillery Guns, 10 Radar Installations, 10 x Helicopters, 30 x Air defence Units, about 300 soft skinned vehicles and 10 x fixed wing aircraft on the ground. A single Army Aviation AH-64 battalion is believed to have destroyed 40 x APCs and over 100 x MBT in an engagement that lasted over 3 hours, firing 107 Hellfire missiles and over 300 x 70mm rockets.

At the very beginning of the war 8 x AH-64 each equipped with 8 x Hellfire, 76 x 70mm rockets and 1,100 rounds of 30mm ammunition attacked radar early warning installations about 80-100 kms inside Iraq. Their task was to open a 30km wide sterilised air corridor through which allied aircraft could transit to targets deep inside enemy territory. During the operation the helicopters fired 27 x Hellfire missiles, 100 rockets and about 4,000 rounds of 30mm ammunition, and achieving a very high success rate over a total distance of some 1,300 kms during the 15 hour mission.

What we are looking at is the natural progression of cavalry operations into another dimension. The 1980s aphorism, 'Rotors are to tracks as tracks were to horses', has not yet quite come to pass. Tracks, machine guns, and barbed wire drove horses from the modern battlefield. However, as the 20th century draws to a close, tanks, APCs, and other tracked vehicles are still very prominent and viable on that battlefield. Just as armour is most effective when supported by infantry, artillery, and even tactical air, helicopters are most effective when used in conjunction with, rather than in place of, armour and the other combat arms. However, helicopters so increase the range, mobility, reach, and vision of armoured forces, that they may be thought of as the latest manifestation of cavalry.

Cavalry operations used to be thought of as light or heavy. In classic cavalry operations, heavy cavalry, as manifested by the mounted man-at-arms or Murat's Cavalry Corps, delivered shock and exploited penetrations. Confederate General JEB Stuart's operations in the first two years of the American Civil War typify light cavalry as a scouting and screening force. Lt Col Banastre Tarrelton's destruction of the defeated Carolina militia after the Battle of Cowpens, during the American War of Independence illustrates light cavalry in pursuit, while his less successful efforts against Francis Marion show some of the limitations in using light cavalry to control insurgents.

Indeed, the division persisted into armoured operations. Heavy armour provided shock, penetration, and exploitation or pursuit, while scouting, screening, and the control of insurgents were the province of light armour. Attack or combat helicopters are roughly analogous to heavy cavalry. Their heavy armament provides shock and limits the enemy's freedom of operation, while their defensive and protective features enable them to operate in the thick of the modern battlefield or strike deep behind enemy lines. Lighter helicopters, while often armed, lack the survivability of their heavier brethren. Consequently, they must operate from concealment or from behind friendly lines. Thus, they inherit the light cavalry roles of scouting and observation.

However, it would be wise to take all of these recent changes in their turn and not go overboard on any one particular system. The attack helicopter is going to be an increasingly important battlefield system in the years to come, but it is part of an essential military whole and not a battle winner in isolation.

In its turn the helicopter is already threatened. To ensure survival helicopters fly close to the nap of the earth (NOE) and hide behind features such as woods and small hills. The race is on to produce effective anti-helicopter mines that recognise friend from foe, and either destroy low flying helicopters operating along likely transit routes, or force them to fly higher where they become vulnerable to missiles and anti-aircraft fire. Plans for large procurements of anti-helicopter mines are already in place in the US and many European Union (EU) nations.

We believe that there are approximately 11,700 helicopters, armed to some degree, in current world service. Of these, about 4,200 may be classed as attack helicopters.

AAC Attack Helicopter

The current attack helicopter in service with the AAC is Lynx with TOW, and will continue to be so until 2000 which is the in service date (ISD) for the British Army's new attack helicopter.

During July 1995 the UK MoD announced the purchase of 67 x Westland WAH-64D Apaches at a cost of £2.5 billion. The WAH-64D was chosen in preference to the European Tiger alternative from British Aerospace and the lower-cost Cobra Venom offer from GEC-Marconi Avionics.

The aircraft, an improved McDonnel Douglas AH64 is to be powered by Rolls-Royce Turbomeca RTM322 engines, giving commonality with the Royal Air Force and Royal Navy EH 101 helicopters.

It is believed that an air-to-air weapon capability will continue to be investigated and trials of the Shorts Starstreak missile onboard an AH-64 will continue in the USA until early 1997. Any longer term decision to proceed will be based on the results of these US Army trials.

The WAH64D will be deployed with two AAC Regiments supporting two divisions, 24 Airmobile Brigade and the Royal Marines. It is probable that about 3,000 jobs will be created in the UK as a result of the purchase.

Support Helicopters

The majority of the troop lift and logistical support for military operations is provided by the RAF who currently operate approximately 130 support helicopters (Wessex, Puma, Chinook). This is a slightly unusual arrangement and there are excellent reasons to support proposals which suggest that these aircraft should be under AAC command and control. This system may not work as well as it might because of differences in operational procedures linked to traditional service attitudes and priorities. We firmly believe that an army commander on the ground should command all the battlefield assets at his disposal including troop lift helicopters and their crews. The British Army is the one remaining major NATO Army where the Army Commander does not have total command and control over his helicopter fleet. Allowing such a situation to continue to exist could invite confusion in a crisis situation.

AAC Regimental Organisation

Organisations for the individual AAC Regiments appear to have settled following the Options for Change Review. The following wiring diagram outlines the organisation of a 3 Regiment AAC in early 1995. 3 Regiment supports the Colchester based 24 Airmobile Brigade. Various regimental organisations are a variation on this theme.

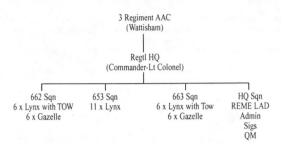

```
                          3 Regiment AAC
                           (Wattisham)
                                |
                            Regtl HQ
                     (Commander-Lt Colonel)
    _____|_____
    |                |                    |                  |
662 Sqn          653 Sqn              663 Sqn            HQ Sqn
6 x Lynx with TOW  11 x Lynx          6 x Lynx with Tow   REME LAD
6 x Gazelle                           6 x Gazelle         Admin
                                                          Sigs
                                                          QM
```

Totals: Approx 450 personnel
        35 Helicopters

Notes:

(1) A Regiment of this type could act as the core formation of an airborne battlegroup. If necessary an infantry aviation company consisting of 3 x rifle platoons and a Milan anti-tank platoon will be attached. The infantry could be moved in RAF Chinooks or Pumas.

(2) 4 Regiment AAC joined 3 Regiment in Wattisham during early 1995 and we believe that both regiments have a similar organisation. Wattisham is also the home of 7 Bn REME - a unit configured as an aircraft workshops. First indications are that the WAH64D will be deployed with both of these regiments.

RAF Support

As previously mentioned the second agency that provides aviation support for the Army is the Royal Air Force. In general terms the RAF provides helicopters that are capable of moving troops and equipment around the battlefield, and fixed wing fighter ground attack (FGA) aircraft that provide close air support to the troops in the vicinity of the Forward Edge of the Battlefield Area (FEBA). The RAF also provides the heavy air transport aircraft that will move men and material from one theatre of operations to another.

```
                    RAF Support Available in the UK
    _____|_____
    |                      |                               |
Wittering               Odiham                        Aldergrove
    |                      |                               |
1 Sqn - Harrier(15)    7 Sqn - Chinook (16)          72 Sqn - Wessex (13)
                       33 Sqn - Puma (10)            230 Sqn - Puma (13)

            Lyneham                        Brize Norton

       24 Sqn - Hercules (11)          10 Sqn - VC10 (8)
       30 Sqn Hercules (11)            216 Sqn - Tristar (8)
       47 Sqn - Hercules (12)
       70 Sqn - Hercules (11)
```

(1) Figures in brackets are our estimate of the number of aircraft in each squadron during early 1997.

(2) A further 18 x Harrier are available with the Operational Conversion Unit (OCU) at RAF Wittering. This OCU has the mobilisation title of 20 (R) Sqn.

(3) Not shown on the above diagram but available for support if necessary are 24 x Tornado GR1A and 30 x Jaguar GR1A/B.

RAF Support Available
British Forces Germany
2 Group RAF

Laarbruch	Bruggen
3 Sqn Harrier (15)	9 Sqn - Tornado GR1 (12)
4 Sqn - Harrier (15)	14 Sqn - Tornado GR1 (12)
18 Sqn - Chinook (5)	17 Sqn - Tornado GR1 (12)
& Puma (4)	31 Sqn - Tornado GR1 (12)

Note: Figures in brackets are our estimate of the number of aircraft in each squadron during early 1997. RAF Laarbruch closes in 1999 and RAF Bruggen in 2002. Aircraft at both of these bases will be returned to the UK.

We would expect the AAC armed helicopter to deal with the localised armoured threats to a British force on operations, with RAF aircraft being used on targets of regimental size (90 tanks) and above. However, high performance modern aircraft are very expensive and fast-jet pilots take up to 3 years to train. It would only be sensible to risk such valuable systems when all other options had failed. In addition, the strength of enemy air defences would probably allow only one pass to be made over the target area. A second pass by fixed wing aircraft after ground defences had been alerted would be almost suicidal.

AAC Aircraft

Lynx AH - Mark 1/7/9

(126 in service). Length Fuselage 12.06m: Height 3.4m: Rotor Diameter 12.8m: Max Speed 330kph: Cruising Speed 232kph: Range 885km: Engines 2 Rolls-Royce Gem 41: Power 2 x 850 bhp: Fuel Capacity 918 litres(internal): Weight (max take off) 4,763kg: Crew one pilot, one air-gunner/observer: Armament 8 x TOW Anti-Tank Missiles: 2-4 7.62mm machine guns: Passengers-able to carry 10 PAX: Combat radius approx 100kms with 2 hour loiter.

Lynx is the helicopter currently used by the British Army to counter the threat posed by enemy armoured formations. Armed with 8 x TOW missiles the Lynx is now the mainstay of the British armed helicopter fleet. However, in addition to its role as an anti-tank helicopter, Lynx can be used for fire support using machine guns, troop lifts, casualty evacuation and many more vital battlefield tasks.

During hostilities we would expect Lynx to operate on a section basis, with 2 or 3 Lynx aircraft armed with TOW directed by a Section Commander possibly flying in a Gazelle. The Section Commander would control what is in reality an airborne tank ambush and following an attack on enemy armour decide when to break contact. Having broken contact, the aircraft would return to a forward base to refuel and rearm. Working from forward bases, some of which are within 10kms of the FEBA, it is suggested that a Lynx section could be turned around in less than 15 minutes. Lynx with TOW replaced SCOUT with SS11 as the British Army's anti-tank helicopter.

We believe the majority of Lynx in British service to be Lynx Mark 7 and that there are currently 24 Lynx Mark 9 (the latest version) in the inventory.

Lynx is known to be in service with France, Brazil, Argentina, The Netherlands, Qatar, Denmark, Norway, West Germany and Nigeria. The naval version carries anti-ship missiles.

TOW 2B

(Tube Launched, Optically Tracked, Wire Guided, Anti-Tank Missile). Length 1.17m: Diameter 15cm: Maximum Range 3750m: Speed 1127khp (200mps): Warhead 3.9kg shaped charge high explosive HEAP : MissileWeight 28.1kg:Guidance utomatic comand to lineof sight: Armour Penetration 800mm.

TOW is the US system that has been adopted for use on the Lynx anti-tank helicopter. First seen in US service in 1965, TOW is a very powerful system that can defeat the armour on all conventional MBTs. It is also a second generation missile in that the operator no longer flies the missile to the target using a control stick. All the operator needs to do is keep the aiming mark on the target and the guidance system will do the rest. AAC Lynx are fitted with the roof-mounted stabilised M65 sight.

TOW 2B is the top attack version of the missile system and these systems in AAC service are being upgraded under the Further Improved Tow Programme which enhances both range (possibly 5,000m) and armour penetration.

Gazelle

(168 in service). Fuselage Length 9.53m: Height 3.18m: Rotor Diameter 10.5m: Maximum Speed 265kph: Cruising Speed 233kph: Range 670km: Engine Turbomeca/RollsRoyce Astazou 111N: Power 592shp: Fuel Capacity 445 litres: Weight 1,800kg (max take off): Armament 2 x 7.62mm machine guns (not a standard fitting).

Gazelle is the general purpose helicopter in use by the AAC and it is capable of carrying out a variety of battlefield roles. Gazelle is a French design built under licence by Westland Aircraft. Over 1,000 Gazelles are in service with air forces and civil aviation organisations throughout the world.

A-109

(5 in service) Fuselage Length 10.7m: Rotor Diameter 11.0m: Cruising Speed 272kph: Range 550kms: Service Ceiling 4570m: Engines 2 x 420-shp Allison 250-C20B turboshafts: Fuel Capacity 560 litres: Weight 1,790kg: Max Take Off Weight 2600 kg: Crew Pilot plus observer + 7 pax:

The AAC has five of these light general purpose aircraft for liaison flying and special tasks. The aircraft are part of 8 Flight based at Netheravon in Wiltshire.

BN-2 Islander

(7 In Service) Crew 2; Length Overall 12.37m; Max Take Off Weight 3,630 kg; Max Cruising Speed at 2,135m (7,000 ft and 75% of power) 257kph (154mph); Ceiling 4,145m (13,600m); Range at 2,137m (7,000ft and 75% of power) 1,153km (717 miles); Range with Optional Tanks 1,965kms (1,221 miles).

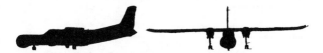

The AAC's BN-2 Islanders carry the Thorn EMI CASTOR (Corps Airborne Stand Off Radar) that is designed to provide intelligence information in the forward edge of the battlefield (FEBA) and beyond while operating well within friendly territory. The radar, located in the nose cone of the aircraft has a 360 degree scan and offers wide coverage against moving and static targets.

Chipmunk T Mark 10

(21 In Service) Crew 2; Length 7.8m; Span 10.3m; Height 2.13m; Max Speed 222 km/ph (138mph); Engine 1 x 1DH Gipsy Major 8 Piston Engine.

The world famous Chipmunk is currently used to give air experience/basic flying training to potential AAC pilots. These aircraft were initially taken into service with the RAF in 1950 and we are sure that it will be some considerable time before they disappear from service. At the height of the Cold War the RAF's permanent presence in Berlin was a flight of 2 x Chipmunks, a presence that we are assured was not directly responsible for the collapse of the Warsaw Pact.

Longbow Apache (WAH-64D)

(67 On Order) Gross Mission Weight 7,746 kgs (17,077 lb; Cruise Speed at 500 meters 272 kph; Maximum Range (Internal Fuel with 20 minute reserve) 462 kms; General Service Ceiling 3,505 meters (11,500 ft); Crew 2; Carries 16 x Hellfire II missiles (range 6,000 meters approx); 76 x 2.75 rockets; 1,200 30mm cannon rounds; 4 x Air to Air Missiles; Engines 2 x Rolls Royce RTM332.

The UK MoD ordered 67 Longbow Apache from Westland during mid 1995 with an ISD at the end of the decade. From this figure of 67 aircraft we believe that there will be 48 aircraft in two regiments (each of 24 aircraft). The remaining 19 aircraft will be used for trials, training and a war maintenance reserve (WMR).

RAF Aircraft

Puma

In Service With:

18 Sqn	RAF Laarbruch
33 Sqn	RAF Odiham
230 Sqn	RAF Aldergrove
OCU	RAF Odiham

(42 in Service) Crew 2 or 3; Fuselage Length 14.06m; Width 3.50m; Height4.38m; Weight (empty) 3,615kg; Maximum Take Off Weight 7,400kgs; Cruising Speed 258 km/ph (192mph); Service Ceiling 4,800m; Range 550kms; 2 x Turbomecca Turmo 111C4 turbines.

The "package deal" between the UK and France on helicopter collaboration dates back to February 1967 when Ministers of the two countries signed a Memorandum of Understanding (MOU). The programme covered the development of three helicopter types - the Puma, Gazelle and Lynx. The main contractors engaged on the programme were Westland and SNIAS for the airframe, and Rolls Royce and Turbomeca for the engines.

Development of the Puma was already well advanced in France when collaboration began. However, the flight control system has been developed jointly by the two countres, and a great deal of work done by Westland to adapt the helicopter for the particular operational requirements of the RAF. Production of the aircraft was shared between the two countries, the UK making about 20% by value of the airframe, slightly less for the engine as well as assembling the aircraft procured for the RAF. Deliveries of the RAF Pumas started in 1971.

The Puma is powered by 2 x Turbomeca Turmo 111C4 engines mounted side by side above the main cabin. Capable of many operational roles Puma can carry 16 fully equipped troops, or 20 at light scales. In the casualty evacuation role (CASEVAC), 6 stretchers and 6 sitting cases can be carried. Underslung loads of up to 3,200kgs can be transported over short distances and an infantry battalion can be moved using 34 Puma lifts.

Chinook

In Service With:

7 Sqn	RAF Odiham
18 Sqn	RAF Laarbruch
27 Sqn (R) (OCU)	RAF Odiham
78 Sqn	RAF MPA (Falklands)

(35 in Service) Crew 3; Fuselage Length 15.54m; Width 3.78m; Height 5.68m; Weight (empty) 10,814kgs; Internal Payload 8,164kgs; Rotor Diameter 18.29m; Cruising Speed 270 km/h (158mph); Service Ceiling 4,270m; Mission Radius(with internal and external load of 20,000kgs including fuel and crew) 55kms; Rear Loading Ramp Height 1.98m; Rear Loading Ramp Width 2.31m; Engines 2 x Avco Lycoming T55-L11E turboshafts.

The Chinook is a tandem-rotored, twin-engined medium lift helicopter. It has a crew of four (pilot, navigator and 2 x crewmen) and is capable of carrying 45 fully equipped troops or a variety of heavy loads up to approximately 10 tons. The first Chinooks entered service with the RAF in 1982. The triple hook system allows greater flexibility in load carrying and enables some loads to be carried faster and with greater stability. In the ferry configuration with internally mounted fuel tanks, the Chinook's range is over 1,600 kms (1,000 miles). In the medical evacuation role the aircraft can carry 24 x stretchers.

Chinook aircraft are currently being upgraded to the HC2 standard. The first of the 32 aircraft being upgraded was delivered to the RAF in the Spring of 1993, with the remaining aircraft were modified by the end of 1995. The HC2 upgrade, for which a total of £145 million was allocated (£53 million during 1993/94), allowed for the aircraft to be modified to the US CH47D standard with some extra enhancements. These enhancements include fitting infra-red jammers, missile approach warning indicators, chaff and flare dispensers, a long range fuel system and machine gun mountings.

This is a rugged and reliable aircraft. During the Falklands War reports suggest that, at one stage 80 fully equipped troops were carried in one lift and, during a Gulf War mission a single Chinook carried 110 Iraqi POWs. The Chinook mid-life update significantly enhances the RAF's ability to support the land forces during the next 25 years.

Between 1 April 1990 and 1 April 1995 the RAF Chinook fleet had flown some 44,200 hours during which time the operating costs (personnel, fuel and maintenance) have been £232 million, a figure that results in a cost of £5,248 per flying hour.

There are currently (late 1996) 35 x Chinook HC Mk2 in the RAF fleet and this figure will rise to 49 when 14 x HC Mk3 aircraft (currently on order) are delivered. The in service date for these new aircraft is late 1997. A further 22 x EH101 support helicopters have been ordered with an in service date of 2000.

Westland Wessex Mark 2

(59 in service - possibly 30 earmarked for Army support). Crew 1-3; Pax 16 in main cabin: Length 20.03m: Main Rotor Diameter 17.07m: Height 4.93m: Cabin Door Size 1.22m x 1.22m: Operating Weight Mk2 3,767kg: Payload Mk2 1,117kg: Max Speed 212kph: Cruising Speed 195kph: Max Range 770km.

The first production model of the Wessex Mk2 was delivered to the RAF in 1962, and until the introduction of Puma the Wessex Mk 2 was the most numerous transport helicopter in service with the British Forces. It is believed that the RAF now operates one Wessex Mk2 squadron which supports UKLF (72 Sqn RAF Aldergrove - 15 aircraft), a Wessex squadron in service with the RAF in Cyprus (No 84 Sqn - RAF Akrotiri - possibly 5/6 aircraft) and another in Hong Kong (28 Sqn - RAF Sek Kong - 8 aircraft). Other marks of Wessex are used by the RAF for Search and Rescue and by the Royal Navy for antisubmarine warfare.

Harrier

In service With:

1 Sqn	RAF Wittering
3 Sqn	RAF Laarbruch
4 Sqn	RAF Laarbruch
20 Sqn (R) OCU*	RAF Wittering

* There appear to be a mix of aircraft at the OCU. We believe that there could be Harrier GR3, GR5/7 and up to 10 x Harrier T4.

Crew (GR 5/7) 1; (T Mark 4 & 4A) 2; Length (GR 5/7) 14m; Length (T Mark 4 & 4A) 17m; Wingspan (normal) 9.3m; Height (GR 5/7) 3.45m; Height (T Mark 4 & 4A) 4.17m; Max Speed 1083 km/ph (673mph) at sea level; All Up Operational Weight approx 13, 494kgs; Armament 2 x 30mm Aden guns, 4 x wingweapon pylons and 1 x underfuselage weapon pylon, conventional or cluster bombs; Engine 1 x RollsRoyce Pegasus 11-21; Ferry Range 5,382 kms (3,310 miles) with 4 x drop tanks.

Capable of taking off and landing vertically, the Harrier is not tied to airfields with long concrete runways but can be dispersed to sites in the field close to the forward edge of the battle area. The normal method of operation calls for a short take off and vertical landing (STOVL), as a short ground roll on take off, enables a greater weapon load to be carried. The Harrier GR3 was the mark of the aircraft that was taken into service in large numbers starting in 1969.

The Harrier GR5 entered service in 1988 with the intention of replacing all of the RAF's GR3's on a one for one basis. However, the GR5 has been upgraded to the GR7, which in turn entered service in June 1990. All three of the operational Harrier squadrons have been equipped with the GR7 and all of the GR3s and GR5s have either been upgraded or withdrawn from service. The differences in the GR5 and the GR7 are mainly in the avionics. The GR7 is equipped with the Forward Looking Infra Red (FLIR) equipment which, when combined with the night vision goggles (NVGs) that the pilot will wear, gives the GR7 a night, low level, poor weather capability. There are small differences in the cockpit layout of the two aircraft including layout and internal lighting standards. In most other respects, the GR7 is similar to the GR5.

The GR5/7 offers many advantages to over the GR3. It possesses the capability to carry approximately twice the weapon load over the same radius of action, or the same weapon load over a much increased radius. In addition it carries a comprehensive ECM (Electronic Counter Measures) suite which can operate in the passive or active mode and will greatly enhance the GR5/7s chances of survival in today's high threat environment. The GR5/7 also has an inertial navigation system that is significantly more effective than that of the GR3.

C-130 Hercules

In Service With:

24 Sqn	RAF Lyneham
30 Sqn	RAF Lyneham
47 Sqn	RAF Lyneham
70 Sqn	RAF Lyneham
57 Sqn (R) OCU	RAF Lyneham

Note: The LTW (Lyneham Transport Wing) appears to have a total of 54 aircraft. Crew 5; Capacity 92 troops or 62 paratroops or 74 medical litters or 19,686kgs of freight; Length 29.78m; Span 40.41m; Height 11.66m; Weight Empty 34, 287kgs; Max Load 45, 093kgs; Max speed 618 km/ ph (384mph); Service Ceiling 13,075m; Engines 4 x Allison T-56A-15 turboprops.

The Hercules C1 is the workhorse of the RAF transport fleet. It has proved to be a versatile and rugged aircraft, primarily intended for tactical operations, including troop carrying, paratrooping, supply dropping and aeromedical duties. The Hercules can operate from short unprepared airstrips, but also possesses the endurance to mount long range strategic lifts if required. The aircraft is a derivative of the C-130E used by the United States Air Force, but is fitted with British Avionic equipment, a roller-conveyor system for heavy air-drops and with more powerful engines. The crew of five includes, pilot, co-pilot, navigator, air engineer and air loadmaster.

As a troop carrier, the Hercules can carry 92 fully armed men, while for airborne operations 62 paratroops can be dispatched in two simultaneous "sticks" through the fuselage side doors. Alternatively, 40 paratroops can jump from the rear loading ramp. As an air ambulance the aircraft can accommodate 74 stretchers.

Freight loads that can be parachuted from the aircraft include: 16 x 1 ton containers or 4 x 8,000 pound platforms or 2 x 16,000 pound platforms or 1 x platform of 30,000 pounds plus. Amongst the many combinations of military loads that can be carried in an air-landed operation are: 3 x Ferret scout cars plus 30 passengers or 2 x Land Rovers and 30 passengers or 2 x Gazelle helicopters.

Of the original 66 C1 aircraft, some 31 have been given a fuselage stretch producing the Mark C3. The C3 stretched version provides an additional 37% more cargo space. Refuelling probes have been fitted above the cockpit of both variants and some have received radar warning pods under the wing tips. One aircraft, designated Mark W2, is a special weather version and is located at the DRA Farnborough.

Current plans appear to be for the replacement of the RAF's ageing 1960s Hercules fleet during the next ten years and during 1995 the UK MOD announced the purchase of 25 x C-130J from US company Lockheed. This aircraft has improved engines, a new glass cockpit with flat screen displays and a two man crew. Production models were available from early 1997.

Orders for a second batch of 30 transport aircraft are believed to be in the system towards the end of the decade and the contenders will probably be Lockheed once again with a C-130 built to a new K standard, and the FLA (future large aircraft). The FLA which will be built by the Rome based Euroflag Consortium, will probably be ready for service from about 2004 and could be capable of carrying a maximum payload of 30 tons as opposed to the 20 tons of the C-130J. British Aerospace is a member of Euroflag consortium.

The most commonly quoted argument in favour of the FLA is that this aircraft could carry a 25 ton payload over a distance of 4,000kms. Thus it is argued that a fleet of 40 x FLA could carry a UK Brigade to the Gulf within 11.5 days, as opposed to the 28.5 days required to make a similar deployment with 40 x C-130s.

Over 1,000 x C-130 have been manufactured and 467 are in service with the US Armed Forces.

Tristar

(8 in service) Crew 3; Passengers 265 and 35,000 pounds of freight; Length 50.05m; Height 16.87m; Span 47.35m; Max Speed 964 km/ph (600mph); Range 6,000 miles (9,600 kms); Engines 3 x 22,680kgs thrust Rolls Royce RB 211524B4 turbofans.

The Tristar K1 and KC1 are strategic tanker conversions of the Lockheed L-1011-500 Tristar commercial airliner. The Tristar K1 can also be fitted with up to 204 passenger seats for the trooping role. The Tristar KC1 tanker/freight aircraft have a large 140 x 102 inch, cargo door and a roller conveyer system capable of accepting up to 20 cargo pallets or seating for up to 196 passengers. Linked pallets can be used to permit the carriage of vehicles.

Also in service is the Tristar C2. This aircraft can carry 265 passengers and 35,000 pounds of freight over ranges in excess of 4,000 miles. It is planned to give these aircraft a tanker capability by fitting two wing refuelling pods.
The Tristar normally cruises at 525mph and with a payload of 50,000 pounds has a range in excess of 6,000 miles. The aircraft entered service in early 1986 with No 216 Sqn which reformed at RAF Brize Norton on 1 Nov 1984.

VC-10

(14 in service with 10 Sqn and 101 Sqn) Crew 4; Carries 150 passengers or 78 medical litters; Height 12.04m; Span 44.55m ; Length 48.36m; Max Speed (425 mph); Range 7596kms; All Up Operational Weight 146,513kgs; Engines 4 x Rolls Royce Conway turbofans.
The VC-10 is a fast transport aircraft which is the backbone of Strike Command's long-range capability, providing flexibility and speed of deployment for British Forces. This multi-purpose

aircraft can be operated in the troop transport, freight and aeromedical roles in addition to maintaining scheduled air services.

The VC-10 carries a flight deck crew of four; captain, co-pilot, navigator and engineer - and has a flight deck seat for an additional supernumerary crew member. Normal cabin staff are two air loadmasters and two air stewards. On scheduled services up to 126 passengers are carried. Under the floor of the aircraft are two large holds which can carry up to 8.5 tons of freight. If necessary, the aircraft can be converted for use as a freighter or an air ambulance when 78 stretcher cases can be carried. Five aircraft are used as airborne refuelling tankers.

CHAPTER 8 ENGINEERS

Corps of Royal Engineers

The engineer support for the Army is provided by the Corps of Royal Engineers (RE). This large corps, currently composed of 21 regiments filled with highly skilled tradesmen, is presently organised as follows:

	Germany	UK
Engineer Regiments	4	4
EOD Regiment	-	1
Resident N Ireland Regiment	-	1
Training Regiments	-	2
TA Engineer Regiments	-	9

There are also a number of independent engineer squadrons world-wide. The former Gurkha Engineer Regiment QGE (Queen's Gurkha Engineers) has now been reduced to a large squadron.

The Royal Engineers provide specialist support to the combat formations, and engineer detachments, can be found at all levels from the Combat Team/Company Group upwards. Combat Engineers could be expected to be involved in the following tasks during specific phases of warfare:

a. Defence: Construction of field defences; minelaying; improvement and construction of obstacles.

b. Attack: Obstacle crossing; demolition of enemy defences (bunkers etc); mine clearance; bridge or ferry construction.

c. Advance: Building or strengthening roads and bridges; removal of booby traps; mine clearance; airfield construction; supply of water; survey.

d. Withdrawal: Demolition of airfields, roads and bridges, fuel ammunition and food dumps, railway tracks and rolling stock, industrial plant and facilities such as power stations; route clearance; minelaying; booby trapping likely enemy future positions and items that might be attractive to the enemy.

Some of the other tasks performed by the men of the RE include map making and survey, the disposal of unexploded munitions (enemy bombs etc), airfield damage repair and advice to other arms on camouflage and concealment. Often amongst the first soldiers into battle, and still involved in dangerous tasks such as Explosive Ordnance Disposal (EOD) and mine clearance in the former Yugoslavia, the Sappers can turn their hands to almost any engineering related task.

Recent peacekeeping tasks have highlighted the importance of combat engineers in all spheres of military activity. During the period 1993-1997 the multitude of tasks for which engineer support was requested stretched the resources of the Corps to its limit. Engineers are almost always among the first priorities in any call for support: tracks must be improved, roads built, accommodation constructed for soldiers and refugees, and clean water provided. All of these are tasks that soak up large amounts of manpower and at the end of 1996, Engineer Regiments were faced with an interval of about 10 months between operational tours with some members of the Corps on their third operational tour in the Former Yugoslavia.

Organisations

The smallest engineer unit is the Field Troop which is usually commanded by a Lieutenant and consists of approximately 44 men. In an Armoured Division, a Field Troop will have up to four sections, each mounted in an APC. Engineer Regiments in UK may have only three sections and may be mounted in wheeled vehicles such as Land Rovers and 4 Ton Trucks. An engineer troop will deploy with most of its equipment scale (known as G1098), stores and explosives to enable it to carry out its immediate battlefield tasks.

Armoured Divisional Engineer Regiment

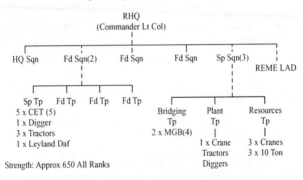

Strength: Approx 650 All Ranks

(1) This Regiment would send most of its soldiers to man the engineer detachments that provide support for a Division's battlegroups; (2) Field Squadron (a Field Squadron will have approximately 68 vehicles and some 200 men; (3) Support Squadron; (4) Medium Girder Bridge; (5) Combat Engineer Tractor; (6) This whole organisation is highly mobile and built around the AFV 432 and Spartan series of vehicles; (7) In addition to the Regimental REME LAD, each squadron has its own REME section of approximately 12 - 15men.

An Engineer Field Troop assigned to work in support of a Battlegroup operating in the area of the FEBA would normally resemble the following:-

Field Troop Organisation

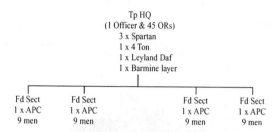

Tp HQ
(1 Officer & 45 ORs)
3 x Spartan
1 x 4 Ton
1 x Leyland Daf
1 x Barmine layer

Fd Sect	Fd Sect	Fd Sect	Fd Sect
1 x APC	1 x APC	1 x APC	1 x APC
9 men	9 men	9 men	9 men

Engineer amphibious capability and specialist support is provided by elements of 28 Engineer Regiment in Germany and a TA Regiment (78 Engineer Regiment with 227 Amph Engr Sqn in the UK. The current organisation of 28 Regiment resembles the following.

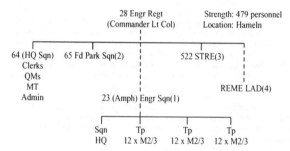

28 Engr Regt
(Commander Lt Col)

Strength: 479 personnel
Location: Hameln

64 (HQ Sqn)
Clerks
QMs
MT
Admin

65 Fd Park Sqn(2)

522 STRE(3)

REME LAD(4)

23 (Amph) Engr Sqn(1)

Sqn HQ	Tp	Tp	Tp
	12 x M2/3	12 x M2/3	12 x M2/3

(1) 23 Amphibious Engineer Squadron, with about 170 men, is believed to have 36 x M2 Ferries (to be replaced by M3 later in the decade); (2) 65 Field Park Squadron acts as the theatre engineering resource unit: as well as manufacturing and repairing equipment, it holds equipment required by all RE units in Germany. The Squadron has about 100 military and 150 civilian staff. (3) 522 Specialist Team Royal Engineers (STRE) is a small unit (approx 26 strong) which provides a design consultancy service for specific engineering tasks. (4) The REME LAD has three repair platoons and a strength of 152 personnel. (5) On mobilisation 28 Engineer Regiment would take 2 x Field Squadrons from 35 Engineer Regiment (also in Hameln) under command, and 21 Field Squadron (EOD) from 33 Engineer Regiment (EOD) in the UK.

The UK Engineer Field Regiment (Regular & TA) is generally a wheeled organisation that would normally have 2 Field Squadrons, a Support Squadron and possibly an Airfield

Damage Repair (ADR) Squadron. Engineer regiments supporting 3(UK) Division are likely to be structured along the lines of the Armoured Divisional Engineer Regiment.

Combat Engineer Tractor

(140 in service) Weight 17, 010kg: Length 7.54m: Height 2.67m: Road Speed 56kph: Road Range 480kms: Fuel Capacity 430 litres: Engine Rolls-Royce C6TCR: Engine Power 320bhp: Crew 2: Armament 1 x 7.62 machine gun.

The Combat Engineer Tractor (CET), which entered service in 1977, is a versatile tracked AFV that can clear obstacles, dig pits, prepare barriers and recover other vehicles that become stuck or damaged. In short, it is an armoured vehicle that can assist in a variety of engineer battlefield tasks, and has an impressive amphibious capability. The 100m winch cable can be fired from the CET by rocket and, using an anchor, can assist in dragging the vehicle up steep slopes and over river banks. CET is found mainly in the Divisional Engineer Regiments and the UK Engineer Regiments. India has 39 x CET in service and Singapore is believed to have another 18.

Replacement plans for the CET are already underway; during 1995 the UK MOD initiated a feasibility study for the next generation Armoured Combat Engineer Vehicle. The new vehicle will be called Terrier and indications are that some 100 vehicles could be required from 2005.

The key Terrier requirements, for a vehicle which could be tracked or wheeled, include the ability to dig, load, grab, lift, carry and winch with the crew under armour protection. The vehicle must also be able to tow a trailer carrying fascines, trackway, the GIAT Viper minefield breaching system; clear scatterable mines; remove or enhance obstacles, and establish routes while keeping pace with other armoured vehicles such as the Challenger 2 MBT and the Warrior MICV.

Chieftain Assault Vehicle Royal Engineers - CHAVRE

The CHAVRE has a crew of 4: the Chieftain gun turret has been removed and replaced by an armoured penthouse upon which the commanders cupola is situated. Mounted over the vehicle structure are two hampers; one at the front of the vehicle and one at the rear. These hampers carry engineer stores such as trackway, fascines or general equipment. A typical hamper load might be 4 x rolls of Class 60 trackway or 3 x fascines.

At the front of the vehicle is a dozer blade or mine plough (either can be used) and at the rear there is a hydraulic winch capable of pulling 10 tons. In the centre of the vehicle is a crane capable of lifting 3.5 tons, with a telescopic jib that extends to 5 metres. A Giant Viper mine clearance explosive hose system can be towed, and the vehicle is armed with an LSW for local defence.

The MOD has ordered 48 vehicles. CHAVRE replaces the Centurion Mk 5 Assault Vehicle Royal Engineers that had been in service since the early 1960s.

The British Army has a requirement for 102 Future Engineer Tanks (FETs) for use by the Royal Engineers, in support of armoured formations operating Vickers Defence Systems Challenger 2 MBTs. It was expected that the UK MoD would specify that existing Challenger 1 or Challenger 2 MBT chassis be used to meet the FET requirement with an in service date after 2005.

Chieftain Bridgelayer (AVLB)

(49 in service) Weight 53, 300kg: Length 13.74m: Height 3.92m: Width 4.16m: Max Road Speed 42kph: Road Range 400km: Engine L60 No4 Mark 7A: Engine Power 730bhp: Fuel Capacity 886 litres: Bridge Length (No. 8 Bridge) 24.4m: Bridge Width (No 8 Bridge)

4.16m: Bridge Weight (No 8 Bridge) 12, 200kg: Crew 3.

In service since 1974 the Chieftain AVLB can carry the No 8 Bridge (24.4m long) and the No 9 Bridge (13m long). A No 8 Bridge can normally be laid across a gap in about 5 minutes. The bridge can then be recovered from the far side of the gap and carried along behind the battlegroup being supported. The main holdings of AVLB are within 32 Engineer Regiment in Germany, with smaller numbers in the UK. The replacement for this vehicle (Future AVLB Gap Crossing Vehicle) will be based on a Challenger chassis and has an in service date of 2001.

M2/3 Ferry

Weight 22,000kg: Length 11.3m: Height 3.58m: Width 2.99m: Width (bridge deployed) 1.42m: Max Road Speed 60kph: Water Speed 15kph: Road Range 1,000kms: Crew 4.

There are approximately 72 x M2 vehicles in British Army service; they are held in 28

Engineer Regiment in Germany and a TA Regiment in the UK. The M2 can be driven into a river and used as a ferry or, when bolted together, form a bridge capable of taking vehicles as heavy as the Challenger MBT. The M2 is a German vehicle which first entered service in 1972; it is expected to be replaced by the M3 Bridge later in the decade.

The M3 has three bridging ramps in place of the four on the M2, a length increase of 2.3 metres, increased buoyancy and can be driven in the water from either end. The vehicle is powered by marine jets instead of propellers and ony 2 x ferries are required to carry an MBT (instead of the 5 x M2's needed for the same task). It is understood that the British Army intends to purchase 50 of these vehicles and that the current cost is in the region of £1 million per vehicle.

Medium Girder Bridge (MGB)

The MGB is a simple system of lightweight components that can be easily manhandled to construct a bridge capable of taking the heaviest AFVs. Two MGBs are held by the Bridging Troop in the Support Squadron of a Divisional Engineer Regiment.

Single span bridge - 30m long which can be built by about 25 men in 45 minutes.

Multi span bridge - a combination of 26.5m spans: a 2 span bridge will cross a 51m gap and a 3 span bridge a 76m gap. If necessary, MGB pontoons can be also be joined together to form a ferry.

During late 1994 a team from 35 Engr Regt set a new world record by building a single storey 9 metre bridge in 10 minutes and 34 seconds. By 1995 the manufacturer Williams Fairey claimed that the MGB was in service with 35 nations world wide. MGB is due to be replaced by the BR90 system (although some MGB will be retained for certain operational requirements).

Class 16 Airportable Bridge

A much lighter bridge than the MGB, the Class 16 can be carried assembled under a Chinook helicopter or in 3 x 3/4 ton vehicles with trailers. A 15m bridge can be constructed by 15 men in 20 minutes. The Class 16 can also be made into a ferry which is capable of carrying the heaviest AFVs.

Giant Viper

Trailer Weight 136kgs; Hose Length 230m; Cleared Zone 83m x 7.3m wide.

The Giant Viper is a system which is used for clearing lanes through a minefield. It consists of a rocket attached to an explosive filled hose, which is carried in a special trailer. The trailer, containing rocket and hose, can be towed behind vehicles such as the CHAVRE, CET or FV 432.

The trailer is positioned 150m from the edge of the minefield and the rocket is fired, propelling the explosive-filled hose into, or right across, the minefield. The subsequent explosion of the hose will breach a lane 180m long and 7.3m wide. Trials and research suggest that in a cleared lane over 90% of anti-tank mines will have been destroyed.

Mine Warfare

Minefields laid by the Royal Engineers will usually contain a mixture of Barmine (anti-tank) and Ranger (anti-personnel). Mk. 7 (antitank) mines may also be used, and anti-disturbance devices may be fitted to some Barmines. Minefields will always be recorded and marked; they should also be covered by artillery and mortar fire to delay enemy mine clearance operations and maximise the attrition of armour. ATGWs are often sited in positions covering the minefield that will give them flank shoots onto enemy armour; particularly the ploughs or rollers that might spearhead a minefield breaching operation.

Barmine (Anti-Tank)

Weight 11kg: Length 1.2m: Width 0.1m: Explosive Weight 8.4kg.

The Barmine is usually mechanically laid by a plough-type trailer that can be towed behind an AFV 432 or Warrior. The Bar Mines are manually placed onto a conveyor belt on the layer from inside the APC. The minelayer automatically digs a furrow, lays the mines into it at the correct spacing and closes the ground over them. Up to 600 mines can be laid in one hour by one vehicle with a 3-man crew. A full width attack (FWAM) fuze and an anti-disturbance fuze are available for Barmine; these are secured on the ends of the mine, adjacent to the pressure plate.

During early 1996 the British Army has announced that it has a requirement to refurbish up to 30,000 L9A1 anti-tank Barmines fitted with the L89A1 pressure fuze. In the longer term, the British Army has a requirement for a Barmine replacement system to meet Staff Requirement (Land) 4036. This requirement includes both the Barmine and an associated command and control system, which could allow the minefield to be switched on and off according to operational requirements. There is an in service date of 2002 for the new system.

Volcano

To meet the British Army Staff Requirement (Land) 4020 for a vehicle-launched scattering anti-tank mine system, during late 1995 the UK MoD selected the Alliant Techsystems M163 Volcano system, with the Alvis Stormer flatbed as the carrier vehicle.

It is believed that the total value of the order is approximately £110 million for 29 x Volcano systems, anti-tank mines, training, spares and the Stormer flatbed carrier. The in service date for the system is 1999.

In British Army service Volcano will only lay anti-tank mines. These mines are carried in canisters, each of which hold six mines, with up to 40 canisters carried on a launcher rack. These are on the rear of the Stormer flatbed and discharge the anti-tank mines either side as the vehicle moves across the terrain. A dispenser control unit provides fire signals, testing and arming of the self-destruct mechanism.

Ranger Mine (Anti-Personnel)

The Ranger Mine is an anti-personnel device which is launched from a projector carried on the top of an AFV 432. This projector can hold 72 tubes, with each tube containing 18 mines. When the tube is fired the mines are scattered in a random pattern up to a distance of 100m. Each mine contains a 10gm charge of RDX, capable of inflicting serious injury to personnel who tread on them. The mine is constructed largely of plastic and incorporates a clockwork arming delay.

Claymore Mine (Anti-Personnel)

Weight 1,58kg: Length 210mm: Width 30mm: Charge Weight 0.68kg.

The Claymore Mine has a curved oblong plastic casing mounted on a pair of bipod legs. The mine is positioned facing the enemy and fired electrically from distances up to 300m away. On initiation, the mine scatters about 700 ball-bearings out to a range of 50m across a 60 degree arc. First purchased from the US in 1963, the Claymore is an effective anti-infantry weapon that is likely to remain in service for many years to come.

Off Route Mine (Anti-Tank)

Length 0.26m: Weight 12kg: Diameter 0.2m: Range 75m. This French mine is designed for vehicle ambush. The mine is placed at the side of the road and a thin electric breakwire laid out across the vehicle's path. The mine is initiated when the vehicle breaks the wire; a shaped charge known as a Misznay Schardin Plate fires an explosively formed projectile into the side of the vehicle.

Mk. 7 Mine (Anti-Tank)

Charge Weight 8.89kg: Mine Weight 13.6kg: Diameter 0.13m.

The Mk. 7 Mine is a large, round metal cased blast mine which may be initiated by pressure or tiltrod (to give it a fullwidth attack capability). It has been in service for many years and, when stocks are exhausted, will be replaced by the Barmine. The Mk. 7 mine can be mechanically laid from a large trailer, akin to a mobile assembly line. This obsolete piece of equipment has a very poor cross-country capability and no protection for the operators.

Mine Detectors

L77A1

Weight Packed with all accessories:	6.5kg
Weight Deployed ready for use:	2.2kg
Approximate Battery Life:	45 hrs
Detection Depth (metal AT mine):	0.6 - 0.7m

The 4C, the standard mine detector of the British Army since 1968, is now being replaced by the Ebinger EBEX420PB. The Army have designated the detector L77A1 and assigned it the NATO Stock Number 6665998693649. The L77A1 is a lightweight modular design which uses pulse induction technologyto locate the metallic content of mines. The battery compartment and electronics are built into the tubular structure, and an audible signal is provided to the operator via a lightweight earpiece. The sensitivity is such that even modern plastic mines with a minimal metallic content can be detected to a depth of 15cm.

BR90 Family of Bridges

In early 1994 the UK MOD announced that the production order had been placed for the BR90 family of bridges that are scheduled to enter service between January 1996 and June 1997 as follows:

January 1996	-	General Support Bridge
November 1996	-	Close Support Bridge
May 1997	-	Two Span Bridge
June 1997	-	Long Span Bridge

Reports during early 1997 indicate that, due to engineering problems the in service date for all four types are slipping and that the complete family of bridges will not be in final service until 1998 at the earliest.

BR90 will be deployed with Royal Engineer units in both Germany and the UK. The production order, valued at approximately £140 million, was issued and accepted in October 1993. This order is believed to have secured up to 250 jobs at the prime contractor, Thompson Defence Projects in Wolverhampton, as well as 50 jobs at Unipower in Watford, plus many other sub-contractors. The components of the system are:

Close Support Bridge - This consists of three tank-launched bridges capable of being carried on the in-service Chieftain bridgelayer and a TBT (Tank Bridge Transporter) truck.

	Weight	Length	Gap
No 10 Bridge	13 tons	26m	24.5m
No 11 Bridge	7.4 tons	16m	14.5m
No 12 Bridge	5.3 tons	13.5m	12m

The existing No 8 and No 9 bridges carried in the Chieftain AVLB will be retained in service.

The Unipower TBT 8 x 8 truck can carry 1 x No 1 Bridge, 1 x No 11 Bridge or 2 x No 12 Bridges.

The TBT has an unladen weight of 21 tons and is also used to transport the General Support Bridge.

General Support Bridge - This system utilises the Automated Bridge Launching Equipment (ABLE) that is capable of launching bridges up to 44 metres in length. The ABLE vehicle is positioned with its rear pointing to the gap to be crossed and a lightweight launch rail extended across the gap. The bridge is then assembled and winched across the gap supported by the rail, with sections added until the gap is crossed. Once the bridge has crossed the gap the ABLE launch rail is recovered. A standard ABLE system set consists of an ABLE vehicle and 2 x TBT carrying a 32 metre bridge set. A 32m bridge can be built by 10 men in about 25 minutes.

Spanning Systems - There are two basic spanning systems. The long span systems allows for lengthening a 32 metre span to 44 metres using ABLE and the two span system allows 2 x 32 metre bridge sets to be constructed by ABLE and secured in the middle by piers or floating pontoons, crossing a gap of up to 60 metres.

CHAPTER 9 - COMMUNICATIONS

"The Japanese airstrike at Pearl Harbour took about 2 hours and the Israeli airstrike in 1967 about 30 minutes to be effective. Some believe that a first strike in cyberspace could cripple a nation's defences in about five minutes. The hackers think otherwise. In the future it could take nano seconds. The hackers believe that in the short term they could be in and out of the C4I networks before current security systems can detect the intrusion.

In military terms the forward edge of the battlefield is known as the FEBA. This new FEBA is already being identified as the CEBA (Cyberic Edge of the Battlefield). If your communicators are not in control of the CEBA, all those billions spent on defence might well be totally wasted."

Defence Briefing in Washington DC - October 1996.

The Royal Corps of Signals

The Royal Corps of Signals (R Signals) provide the communications throughout the command system of the Army. Individual battlegroups are responsible for their own internal communications, but all communications from Brigade level and above are the responsibility of the Royal Signals.

Information is the lifeblood of any military formation in battle and it is the responsibility of the Royal Signals to ensure the speedy and accurate passage of information that enables commanders to make informed and timely decisions, and to ensure that those decisions are passed to the fighting troops in contact with the enemy. The rapid, accurate and secure employment of command, control and communications systems maximises the effect of the military force available and consequently the Royal Signals act as an extremely significant 'Force Multiplier'.

The Royal Corps of Signals provides about 9% of the Army's manpower with 11 Regular and 11 Territorial Army Regiments, each generally consisting of between 3 and up to 6 Sqns with between 600 and 1,000 personnel. In addition, there are 20 Regular and 3 Territorial Army Independent Squadrons, each of which has about 200 men, and 4 Independent Signal Troops of between 10 and 80 men each. Royal Signals personnel are found wherever the Army is deployed including every UK and NATO headquarters in the world. The Headquarters of the Corps is at the Royal School of Signals (RSS) located at Blandford in Dorset.

Royal Signals units based in the United Kingdom provide command and control communications for forces that have operational roles both in the UK itself, including Northern Ireland, and overseas including mainland Western Europe and further afield wherever the Army finds itself. There are a number of Royal Signals units permanently based in Germany, Holland and Belgium from where they provide the necessary command and control communications and Electronic Warfare (EW) support for both the British

Army and other NATO forces based in Europe.

Royal Signals units are also based in Cyprus, the Falkland Islands, Belize and Gibraltar. Regular Army Royal Signals units based in the United Kingdom in support of NATO include:

UK Units Supporting NATO and RJDF Formations

2 Signal Regiment which provides command and Control communications for up to three Divisions in the ARRC including one multinational Division.

3 (UK) Mechanised Division Headquarters and Signal Regiment. This Regiment provides the command and control communications for 3 (UK) Division that deploys as part of the Allied Command Europe (ACE) Rapid Reaction Corps or provides units to the RJDF.

1 (Mechanised) Brigade Signal Squadron. This unit provides communications for the UK Mobile Force (Land) which deploys to Northern Germany and Denmark.

209 Signal Squadron supports 19 (Mechanised) Brigade based in Catterick which is part of the ARRC.

210 (Airmobile) Brigade Signal Squadron provides communications for 24 (Airmobile) Brigade based in Colchester.

216 Parachute Signal Squadron is part of 5th Airborne Brigade which is able to operate either in the UK, within the NATO area of operations or worldwide.

249 (AMF(L)) Signal Squadron provides communications for a multi-national NATO Brigade that deploys to Norway and Denmark or Turkey and Greece.

264 (SAS) Signal Squadron supports the Special Air Service Regiment.

UK Units - Supporting National Defence Formations

Regular Army Royal Signals units based in the UK which are not allocated to NATO include:

11 Signal Regiment stationed at Blandford in Dorset is the administrative unit for the Royal School of Signals (RSS) and carries out basic Trade Training, promotion courses for potential Non Commissioned Officers and basic training for the TA soldiers of the Royal Signals.

15 Signal Regiment provides command and control communications for the security forces in Northern Ireland. This Regiment has 3 Squadrons to support the 3 Brigades in the Province.

30 Signal Regiment which provides communications for all Army and RAF forces that deploy outside the NATO area of operations. This Regiment always maintains troops who

are held on 24 hours notice to move to anywhere in the world. One Squadron of the Queen's Gurkha Signal Regiment is permanently attached to 30 Signal Regiment and serves in the United Kingdom.

Units Deployed Outside the UK

Royal Signals units that are permanently deployed in Europe in support of British and other NATO forces include:

1 (UK) Armoured Division Headquarters and Signal Regiment. This Regiment which has three Armoured Brigade Squadrons provides communications for the Divisional Headquarters and the three Brigades in the 1st (UK) Armoured Division.

7 (ARRC) Signal Regiment provides command and control communications for the ARRC headquarters which involves providing communications to the formation's multi-national Divisions.

14 Signal Regiment (Electronic Warfare) provides the highly sophisticated electronic warfare support for the Headquarters of the ARRC and for the 1st and 3rd (UK) Divisions. In late 1995 14 Signal Regiment returned to the UK where it is stationed at the former RAF base at Brawdy in Wales.

16 Signal Regiment. This Regiment provides communication support for a number of multi-national logistic organisations and fixed communications for British Forces Germany and RAF Germany.

A Royal Signals Regiment is based in Cyprus to support the Army and RAF forces in the Sovereign Base Areas and a Royal Signals Squadron supports the United Nations Force.

TA Units - At 1 Dec 1996

Royal Signals Territorial Army (TA) units include:

11 (ARRC) Signal Brigade based in Liverpool comprises the following units that all deploy to mainland Europe to provide communication for various headquarters in the ARRC.

33rd (Lancashire and Cheshire)Signal Regiment (V) based in Liverpool.
34th (Northern) Signal Regiment (V) based in Middlesbrough.
35th (South Midland) Signal Regiment (V) based in Birmingham.
36th (Eastern)Signal Regiment (V) based in London
55th Signal Regiment (V) based in Liverpool.

The Regular Army's 2 Signal Regiment also comes under the command of 11 Signal Brigade.

2nd (National Communications) Signal Brigade with its headquarters in Corsham is responsible for providing communication for Military Home Defence and operates the Army Fixed Telecommunications System (AFTS). Units include:

31 (Special Task) Signal Regiment(V) based in London.
32 (Scottish) Signal Regiment(V) based in Glasgow.
37 (Wessex and Welsh) Signal Regiment(V) based in Redditch.
38 Signal Regiment(V) based in Sheffield.
71 (Yeomanry) Signal Regiment(V) based in Bexleyheath.
56 Signal Squadron(V) based in Reading.

63 (V) SAS Signal Squadron is an independent unit that provides communication support for the Territorial Army Special Air Service Regiments.

In essence the 11 TA Signals Regiments provide:

3 x Ptarmigan Regiments
2 x Euromux Regiments
6 x National Communications Regiments
3 x Independent Signals Squadrons
2 x Special Communications Squadrons

The 2 (National Communications) Brigade units are being restructured to provide Regional and National Communications support to Land Command. An independent Combat Service Support Group Squadron will also be formed.

Armoured Divisional Signal Regiment Organisation

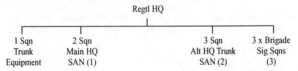

Notes: (1) SAN - Secondary Access Node (2) A Divisional HQ will have two HQs to allow for movement and possible destruction. The main HQ will be setup for approx 24 hrs with the alternate HQ (Alt HQ) set up 20-30 kms away on the proposed line of march of the division. When the Main HQ closes to move to a new location the Alt HQ becomes the Main HQ for another 24 hour period. (3) Expect a Brigade Sig Sqn to have a Radio Troop and a SAN Troop.

R Signals units are currently operating the following types of major equipment:

        Mobile Satellite Terminals
        HF, VHF and UHF Radios
        Radio Relay (carrying telephone & teleprinter links)
        Teleprinters, Fax, CCTV and ADP Equipment
        Computers
        Line

The communications systems used by the Royal Signals include:

Ptarmigan

Ptarmigan is a mobile, secure battlefield system that incorporates the latest technology and has been designed to improve communications reliability, capacity and interoperability.

Built by Siemens-Plessey Christchurch in the mid 1980s Ptarmigan is a user-friendly, computer controlled communications system which was initially designed to meet the needs of the British Army in Germany. The system consists of a network of electronic exchanges or Trunk Switches that are connected by satellite and multi-channel radio relay (TRIFFID) links that provide voice, data, telegraph and fax communications. The Trunk switch, radio and satellite relays together with their support vehicles comprise a 'Trunk Node' and all field headquarters include a group of communications vehicles that contain an Access Switch which can be connected to any Trunk Switch giving access to the system. This ensures that headquarters have exceptional flexibility in both siting and facilities and trunk communications then present no constraints on operations.

Additionally Ptarmigan has a mobile telephone or Single Channel Radio Access (SCRA) which gives isolated or mobile users an entry point into the entire system.

Triffid

Radio relay links within Ptarmigan are provided by TRIFFID which is a radio equipment that has 3 interchangeable radio frequency modules known as 'heads'. Each TRIFFID link carries the equivalent of up to 32 voicecircuits at a data rate of 512 kb/s plus an engineering circuit.

Euromux

EUROMUX is a trunk system manufactured by Racal which is similar in principle to the PTARMIGAN system and is interoperable with the trunk systems of other NATO armies. TRIFFID is used to provide the relay links within the system.

Clansman

Is the name given to the in-service family of tactical radios with which the British Army is currently equipped to provide communications from formation headquarters forward to the fighting units. CLANSMAN is a ligher, far more reliable and adaptable system than the ageing LARKSPUR system that it replaced during the early 1980s. In its turn CLANSMAN will be replaced by BOWMAN.

Clansman Manpack Radios

	Used By	Weight	Range	Freq coverage
PRC 349	Inf Sec	1.5 kg	2km	37-46.975
PRC 350	Inf Pl or Sec	3.6 kg	5km	36-56.975
PRC 351	Coy/Sqn	6.3 kg	8km	30-75.975
PRC 352	Coy/Sqn	9.2 kg	16km	30-75.975
PRC 320	Coy/Pl	11.0 kg	50km	2-29.999

Clansman Vehicle Radios

	Used By	Weight	Range	Freq coverage
VRC 321	Command Nets	23 kg	60km	1.5-29.999
VRC-322	Command Nets	52 kg	80km	1.5-29.999
VRC-353	Bn/Coy/Sqn	22 kg	30km	30-75.975

On the FEBA these Clansman radios are operated by the Battlegroup Signal Platoons but further back (generally Brigade level and backwards towards Divisional, Corps and Army HQ) will be the responsibility of the Royal Signals.

Bowman

Bowman is a tactical communications system that has been designed to provide a replacement for the series of Clansman radios currently in service with the British Army. Bowman will almost certainly make use of the latest packet radio technology and an original project demonstrator contract for a 25 station system was awarded to Racal-BCC in 1988. Current plans are for an in service date of 2001.

There now appear to be two serious contenders for the contract:-

Racal Radio/Siemens Plessey	-	Yeoman Syste
ITT/ BAe/Hunting/N Telecom	-	Crossbow System

During mid 1996 there were indications that the MoD is planning an overhaul of the programme and is about to incorporate the next generation combat net radio programme into existing plans by accelerating the introduction of a high data-rate transmission capability into the Bowman system, something that was originally planned for a later phase.

During mid 1996 both of the consortia were awarded five-month, £1 million study contracts to enable them to work on systems architecture for integrating the VICDS (Vehicle Integrated Communications and Information Distribution System) into the Bowman system.

This is a significant change for VICDS had originally been planned as a separate procurement invoving a £500 million contract for a local-area-network (LAN) system ith a standardized interface. The UK MoD now has a requirement to increase combat formation headquarters data throughput sooner, to cope with the changed pace of data demands brought about by battlefield digitization. Both of the Bowman contenders now have to define the LAN architecture plus the interface, and are to be responsible for ensuring that their Bowman submissions are capable of working with the system.

A further factor that could complicate the Bowman programme is the parallel requirement to support the British Army's overall digitization effort. This was revealed in the UK Army Digitization Masterplan revealed at the end of 1995. This plan calls for a new Army command and control system operating at all levels from platforms such as armoured vehicles through to the most senior headquarters.

The first stage of this plan calls for the supply of around 400 battle management systems, capable of being used at all levels of command plus the communications equipment necessary to support them. It is believed that trials of this equipment are planned for early 1997.

Note: December 1996 reports suggested that the two consortia had agreed to form a partnership that would allow the ongoing development costs to be virtually halved.

Satellite Communications (SATCOM)

The Royal Signals deploys transportable and manpack satellite ground stations to provide communications links for headquarters or small groups located in remote parts of the world via its SKYNET 4B system. Operations in the Falklands and Namibia proved the value of satellite communications and during the Gulf war there was an extensive use of SATCOM ground terminals particularly the Racal VSC501. It is expected that a new series of SKYNET 5 satellites will be introduced to enhance SATCOM facilities in the future.

Wavell

Wavell is a battlefield automatic data processing computer system, designed to accept information from all the battlefield intelligence agencies, and produce this information on request in hard copy or on a VDU. Information is then used to assist commanders and their staff with the analysis of intelligence and subsequent conduct of operations. Each headquarters from Corps down to Brigade level is equipped with its own Wavell computers that are linked to the PTARMIGAN system

Wavell will almost certainly be continually upgraded during the 1990s with interfaces planned for operation with BATES, ADCIS (Air Defence Command Information System) and Vixen. The integration of Wavell with the German HEROS, French SACRA and US MCS Command and Control system will probably be a high priority.

Slim

SLIM is a new system using the personal computer equipment used in the Gulf war which is being developed to complement WAVELL.

Bates

BATES is a battlefield artillery engagement system which has been designed to centralise the command and control of artillery, with all fire missions being routed through a central control cell and then passed on to the appropriate fire units. Access to the system is available down to the level of artillery FOOs (Forward Observation Officers) who have their own digital entry devices. BATES will eventually replace FACE (Forward Artillery Computing Equipment).

Artillery intelligence entered in the system is available for commanders and their staff through the Wavell interface and much of the routine and logistic tasks are processed by the equipment, thus freeing the staff for other tasks.

BATES is an important part of the MLRS - AS 90 - PHOENIX COBRA series of battlefield fire support systems and when it is finally in service will provide valuable support to these equipments. However, there appears to have been serious delays in bringing BATES into service, and once in service there could be significant teething problems as BATES is integrated with other systems.

We believe that some £50 million has been spent on BATES and that there will eventually be up to 200 systems in operation with the British Army.

Vixen

Vixen has been designed to provide an automated system for processing of electronic intelligence. It will probably be mounted in soft skinned vehicles and deployed with the electronic warfare regiment which amongst its many tasks listens to enemy signal traffic and passes vital intelligence to the operational staff. Vixen became operational in late 1992 and it is probable that the system is linked to the existing electronic direction finding equipment subsequently feeding results into the BATES and Wavell ADP systems. The cost of the Vixen system was believed to be in the region of £36.5 million.

Scimitar

Scimitar has been designed to provide a secure combat net communications system to include a frequency agile ability for use in areas where the ECM threat is high. Equipments are man-portable or vehicle mounted and the system has three basic equipments:

Scimitar H (HF radio)

Freq 1.6 30MHz - 284000 channels Weight 4.0 kgs (manpack).

Scimitar V (VHF vehicle or man-pack radio)

Freq 3088MHz - 2320 channels Weight 4.8 kgs (manpack)

Scimitar M (Pocket sized VHF radio)

Freq 68 - 88MHz - 800 channels - Weight 0.5 kg.

Some Scimitar units are in use with the British Army and it is known to be in use with Jordan, Portugal, Turkey and Sweden. Manufactured by Plessey the average cost of a Scimitar radio is probably in the area of £8,000.

Jaguar

Jaguar is manufactured by Racal Tacticom and is a similar system to Scimitar with the ability to frequency hop in ECM environments. The radio can be used in both the vehicle and manpack roles and the main characteristics are as follows:

Frequency Range	30-88MHz		
Temperature Range	-40 to 70 degrees C		
Weight	5 kgs		
Channels	2320	Spacing	25 kHz

Jaguar is in service with the British Army and US Navy. Over 30 nations are currently using this equipment and sales to date are believed to be in excess of £120 million.

Army Fixed Telecommunications Systems

The peacetime management of the Army depends heavily on effective communications . The Royal Signals Army Fixed Telecommunication System (AFTS) provides all the telephone, telegraph, facsimile, data systems and radio and line links for the Army in the United Kingdom. AFTS is operated and maintained by 2 (National Communications) Brigade and the system serves over 40,000 subscribers. The staff required to operate the AFTS is approximately 1,100 of whom 40% are military personnel who are located all over the UK in six (Fixed Service) Signal Squadrons supported by operational, engineering, planning and co-ordination staff at Headquarters 2 (NC) Brigade at Corsham in Wiltshire.

One of the ADP systems in the UK is MAPPER which stands for Maintenance, Preparation and Presentation of Executive Reports. This system is used both as a peacetime management aid to staffs in major headquarters but also for command and control of Military Home Defence and was expanded for use in the Gulf war when MAPPER stations were deployed to Saudi Arabia and linked back to the United Kingdom. Its success in the Gulf has led to the system being used in post Gulf war operations including the Balkans.

In Germany the Telecommunications Group Headquarters based at Rheindahlen provides a sophisticated fixed communications system based on the Integrated Services Digital

Network (ISDN). Project Rodin, which is intended to modernise the fixed communications system for both the Army and the RAF in Germany will, when introduced, use state of the art digital technology and will be able to interact with other German and British military and civilian networks.

The Communications Projects Division (CPD) provides engineering support for military fixed communications systems worldwide. CPD is part of the Royal School of Signals at Blandford in Dorset.

Digitisation

Digitisation refers to putting the capabilities for digital communications into a platform. Digital modulation is the process of encoding a continuous analog signal into a discontinuous signal. Then numerical codes consisting of discrete on (one) and off (zero) pulses are assigned to represent a measure of the basic signal. The measuring process involves sampling the amplititude of the continuous signal at intervals and transmitting a digital code to represent the amplitude. The same process can be used in data transmissions where digital codes represent letters and numbers. Linking platforms from aircraft to mines and sensors on the ground in an intelligent circuit allows these systems to interact automatically on a continual flow of information around the circuit.

Linked to digitisation, the next trend in communications is probably towards secure image transmission linking information from humans and sensors. For example, a platoon commander's sketch map of the current situation in his area can be transmitted simultaneously to the company, battalion, brigade and divisional headquarters and either modified or confirmed by sensor information. This map could then be scanned into the overall C3I system and both humans and sensors made aware of the results. Time spent in talking about the situation on the air and the possibility of confusion and misunderstandings are dramatically reduced.

CHAPTER 10 - COMBAT SERVICE SUPPORT

> *"It is more important to destroy those places that contain the elements of military power (the magazines and stores) than soldiers, who are nothing without their stores."*
>
> Systeme de Guerre moderne - General Comte de Cessac 1797

> *"Most people do not realize that military logistics can never operate under the civilian maxim of - just in time. To be effective military logistics have to be organised around a different set of priorities better described as - just in case."*
>
> Commander Logistic Support HQ MND (SW) Rear Bosnia 1996

Logistic Support

In the wake of the 1990 Logistic Support Review, the British Army decided that in the future, logistic support will be based upon the twin pillars of service support (the supply chain) and equipment support (the maintenance of equipment).

Combat Service Support within the British Army is now provided by the Royal Logistic Corps (RLC), the Royal Electrical and Mechanical Engineers (REME) and the Royal Army Medical Corps (RAMC).

Within any fighting formation, logistic units from these Corps typically represent about 30% of the manpower total of an Armoured Division, and with the exception of certain members of the RAMC, all are fully trained fighting soldiers.

The task of the logistic units on operations is to maintain the combat units in the field which entails:

a. SUPPLY AND DISTRIBUTION   -   of ammunition, fuel, lubricants, rations and spare parts.

b. RECOVERY AND REPAIR   -   of battle damaged and unserviceable equipment.

c. TREATMENT AND EVACUATION   -   of casualties.

In a Division the commanders of the logistic units all operate from a separate, self contained headquarters under the command of a Colonel who holds the appointment of the Division's Deputy Chief of Staff (DCOS). This headquarters, usually known as the Divisional Headquarters (Rear),coordinates the whole of the logistic support of the Division in battle.

Supplies, reinforcements and returning casualties pass through an area located to the rear of the Division where some of the less mobile logistic units are located. This area is known as the Divisional Admin Area (DAA) and its staff is responsible for coordinating the flow of all materiel and personnel into and out of the Divisional area.

The Royal Logistic Corps (RLC)

The RLC is the youngest Corps in the Army and was formed in April 1993 as a result of the recommendations of the Logistic Support Review. The RLC results from the amalgamation of the Royal Corps of Transport (RCT), the Royal Army Ordnance Corps (RAOC), the Army Catering Corps (ACC), the Royal Pioneer Corps (RPC) and elements of the Royal Engineers (RE). The Corps makes up about 16% of the Army with 16,600 Regular personnel and 10,000 Territorial Army soldiers wearing its cap badge.

The RLC has very broad responsibilities throughout the Army including the movement of personnel throughout the world, the Army's air dispatch service, maritime and rail transport, operational resupply, explosive ordnance disposal which includes the hazardous bomb disposal duties in Northern Ireland and in mainland Britain during the current IRA terrorist campaign, the operation of numerous very large vehicle and stores depots both in the UK and overseas, the training and provision of cooks to virtually all units in the Army, the provision of pioneer labour and the Army's postal and courier service.

The principal field elements of the RLC are the Close Support and the General Support Regiments whose primary role is to supply the fighting units with ammunition, fuel and rations (Combat Supplies).

A division has an integral Close Support Regiment which is responsible for manning and operating the supply chain to Brigades and Divisional units.

Close Support Regiment RLC

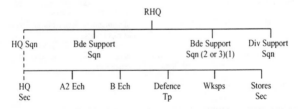

Note:

(1) A regiment could have two or three brigade support sqns depending upon the size of the division being supported.

(2) Some of these regiments may have a Postal and Courier Sqn.

Brigade Support Squadron

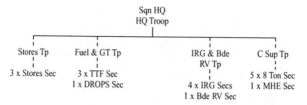

Divisional Support Squadron

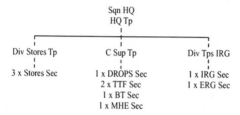

The General Support Regiment's role is primarily to supply ammunition to the Royal Artillery using DROPS vehicles and to provide Tank Transporters that move armoured vehicles more rapidly and economically than moving them on their own tracks.

General Support Regiment RLC

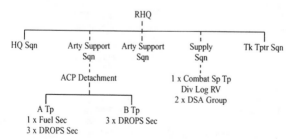

Both types of Regiment have large sections holding stores both on wheels and on the ground. A Division will typically require about 1,000 tons of Combat Supplies a day but demand can easily exceed that amount in high intensity operations.

Battlegroups in contact with the enemy can carry a limited amount of C Sups with them, particularly ammunition, which is replenished from RLC vehicles located immediately to the rear of battlegroups in Immediate Replenishment Groups (IRGs). As the IRG vehicles are emptied they return to the RLC Squadron location and fully loaded replacements are automatically sent forward so that a constant supply is always available to the battlegroup.

Ammunition and spares are generally carried on NATO standard pallets which are loaded to meet the anticipated requirements of particular units and if required, bulk is broken at the IRG location. Fuel is usually carried in bulk fuel tankers (TTFs) which top-up battlegroup vehicles direct. However there is still a requirement for a large number of the traditional jerricans. Much of other fuel is delivered to the forward areas through the NATO Central European Pipeline System (CEPS).

Artillery ammunition constitutes by far the largest single element in the logistic pipeline and the bulk of it is delivered directly to the Royal Artillery guns, rocket and missile launchers by RLC Demountable Rack Off Loading and Pickup System (DROPS) vehicles from the General Support Regiment which are capable of meeting the requirement of even the highest intensity consumption.

Logistic Support in Bosnia

Between 1 Jan and 31 October 1996 the RLC were involved in the following logistic support to British forces in the area.

Ammunition

Tonnage held at 2nd Line	1,488 tons

Petrol, Oil and Lubricants

Litres Drawn	36 million
Disposal of waste oil/fuel	300,000 litres
LPG filled	518,000 kg

Rations

Total issued to units	£8.128 million
Fresh ration issues to units	15,479 pallets

Transport

Total kms travelled	7.050 million
DROPS movements	3,307 kms
TTF movement	448,000 kms
Tank transporter movement	942,000 kms
Armoured vehicle movements	1,608 kms

Movements

Containers received into theatre	1,194
Containers despatched out of theatre	543
Vehicle loads into theatre (40 ft vehicles)	1,170
Loaded rail wagons received	325
Loaded rail waggons dispatched	39
Flights to/from theatre	1,111
Equipment flown into theatre	1,259 million kgs

Materiel

Demands received from units	234,305
Receipts into theatre	5,155,227 kg

Postal

Receipts (surface)	96,000 kg
Receipts (air)	342,000 kg
Despatches (surface)	36,000 kg
Despatches (surface)	63,000 kg
Blueys (received)	2.572 million
Blueys (dispatched)	6.628 million

Laundry & Baths

Laundry washed	249,322 bags
Showers provided	98,582 personnel cleaned

There are some fascinating statistics included in the above list. Blueys are the name given to the lightweight, blue coloured forces airmail letters. The fact that about 2.6 times more letters were written by troops in Bosnia than were received will probably keep a horde of social scientists in employment for some considerable time.

RLC Miscellaneous

Apart from the RLC units that provide direct support the operational formations the RLC is directly responsible for:

Army School of Mechanical Transport - Leconfield
Base Ordnance Depots (Bicester & Donnington)
Base Ammunition Depots (Longtown & Kineton)
Army School of Ammunition (Temple Herdwyke)
Petroleum Centre (West Moors)
Army Base Vehicle Organisation (Ashchurch)
Armoured Vehicle Sub Depot (Ludgershall)
Army School of Catering (Aldershot)
Royal Logistic Corps Training Centre (Deepcut)

Daily Messing Rates

The allowances per day for catering purposes are based on a ration scale costed at current prices and known as the daily messing rate (DMR). The ration scale is the same for all three services, and contrary to popular Army belief the RAF is not supplied with wine etc at public expense. The rate per day is the amount that the catering organisation has to feed each individual serviceman or servicewoman.

The scale is costed to the supply source of the food items. When the source of supply is more expensive due to local conditions the DMR is set higher to take account of local costs. A general overseas ration scale exists for overseas bases and attachments. This scale has a higher calorific value to take into account the conditions of heat, cold or humidity that can be encountered.

Ration scales vary according to location. The home ration scale in the UK is designed to provide 2,900 kilo-calories nett - that is, after loss through preparation and cooking. The general overseas ration scale used in overseas bases, includes an arduous duty allowance, to allow for climate and provides 3,400 kilo-calories nett. In field conditions, where personnel are fed from operational ration packs, 3,800 kilo-calories are provided.

RLC Catering Units feed the Army generally using detachments of cooks attached to units. The following were the daily messing rates (DMR) at the end of 1995:

Army, RAF and RN Shore Establishments	£1.75 per day
RN Ships and Submarines	£1.86 per day
Falkland Islands	£2.03 per day
Cyprus	£1.93 per day
Gibraltar	£2.07 per day

The Royal Electrical & Mechanical Engineers REME

The Logistic Support review of 1990 recommended that Equipment Support should remain separate from the other logistic pillar of Service Support and consequently the REME has retained not only its own identity but expanded its responsibilities. Equipment Support encompasses equipment management, engineering support, supply management, provisioning for vehicle and technical spares and financial management responsibilities for in-service equipment.

The aim of the REME is to keep operationally fit equipment in the hands of the troops and in the current financial environment it is important that this is carried out at the minimum possible cost. The equipment that REME is responsible for ranges from small arms and trucks to helicopters and Main Battle Tanks. All field force units have some integral REME support (1st line support) which will vary, depending on the size of the unit and the equipment held, from a few attached tradesmen up to a large Regimental Workshop of over

200 men. In war REME is responsible for the recovery and repair of battle damaged and unserviceable equipments.

The development of highly technical weapon systems and other equipment has meant that REME has had to balance engineering and tactical considerations. On the one hand the increased scope for forward repair of equipment reduces the time out of action, but on the other hand engineering stability is required for the repair of complex systems. The major changes which have resulted from the Options for Change and Logistic Support Reviews are that four REME Equipment Support Battalions were formed in 1993, to provide second line support for the British contribution to the ACE Rapid Reaction Corps (ARRC) and formations in the UK. Two battalions are based in the UK and three battalions are based in Germany to support 1(UK) Armoured Division. There are five TA REME battalions.

REME Support Battalion

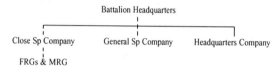

Battalion Headquarters

Close Sp Company   General Sp Company   Headquarters Company

FRGs & MRG

Note: Approx 450 personnel.

The Close Support Company will normally deploy a number of FRG's (Forward Repair Groups) and MRGs (Medium Repair Groups) in support of brigades. The company is mobile with armoured repair and recovery vehicles able to operate in the forward areas, carrying out forward repair of key nominated equipment often by the exchange of major assemblies. It is also capable of carrying out field repairs on priority equipment including telecommunications equipment and the repair of damage sustained by critical battle winning equipments.

The role of the General Support Company is to support the Close Support Companies and Divisional Troops. Tasks include the regeneration of fit power packs for use in forward repair and the repair of equipment backloaded from Close Support Companies. The General Support Company will normally be located to the rear of the divisional area in order to maximise productivity and minimise vulnerability.

In manpower terms the support available to 1(UK) Armoured Division in the ARRC will be somewhere in the area of the following:

Armoured Regiment	120
Armoured Recce Regiment	90
Armoured Infantry Battalion	90

Close Support Engineer Regiment	85
General Support Engineer Regiment	110
Field Regiment Royal Artillery	115
Air Defence Regiment Royal Artillery	160
Army Air Corps Regiment	130
Signals Regiment	60
RLC Close Support Regiment	75
RLC General Support Regiment	95
REME Battalion	450

Medical Services

"Stop dying at once and when you get up, get your bloody hair cut."

Colonel AD Wintle to Trooper Cedric Mayes (Royal Dragoons)

The patient lived for another 40 years.

The Royal Army Medical Corps (RAMC)

In peace, the personnel of the RAMC are based at the various medical installations throughout the world or in field force units and they are responsible for the health of the Army.

On operations, the RAMC is responsible for the care of the sick and wounded, with the subsequent evacuation of the wounded to hospitals in the rear areas. Each Brigade has a field ambulance which is a regular unit that operates in direct support of the battlegroups. These units are either armoured, airmobile or parachute trained. In addition, each division has two field ambulance units that may be regular or TA that provide medical support for the divisional troops and can act as manoeuvre units for the forward brigades when required.

All field ambulance units have medical sections that consist of a medical officer and eight Combat Medical Technicians. These sub-units are located with the battlegroup or units being supported and they provide the necessary first line medical support. In addition, the field ambulance provides a dressing station where casualties are treated and may be resuscitated or stabilised before transfer to a field hospital. These units have the necessary integral ambulance support, both armoured and wheeled to transfer casualties from the first to second line medical units.

Field hospitals may be regular or TA and all are 200 bed facilities with a maximum of 8 surgical teams capable of carrying out life saving operations on some of the most difficult surgical cases. Since 1990 most regular medical units have been deployed on operations either in the Persian Gulf or the former Yugoslavia.

Casualty Evacuation (CASEVAC) is by ambulance, either armoured or wheeled, driven by RLC personnel or by helicopter when such aircraft are available. A Chinook helicopter is capable of carrying 44 stretcher cases and a Puma can carry 6 stretcher cases and 6 sitting cases.

In 1996 there were 12 x field ambulances/ field hospitals in the regular army (3 in Germany and 9 in the UK) plus 18 in the TA. The 1996 personnel total of the RAMC was 2,582.

The Queen Alexandra's Royal Army Nursing Corps (QARANC)

On the 1st April 1992 the QARANC became an all nursing and totally professionally qualified Corps. Its male and female, officer and other rank personnel, provide the necessary qualified nursing support at all levels and covering a wide variety of nursing specialities. QARANC personnel can be found anywhere in the world where Army Medical services are required. The 1996 QARANC personnel total was 951.

Royal Army Dental Corps (RADC)

The RADC is a professional corps that in late 1996 consisted of just over 403 officers and soldiers. The Corps fulfils the essential role of maintaining the dental health of the Army in peace and war, both at home and overseas. Qualified dentists and oral surgeons, hygienists, technicians and support ancillaries work in a wide variety of military units - from static and mobile dental clinics to field medical units, military hospitals and dental laboratories.

The Adjutant General's Corps (AGC)

The Adjutant General's Corps formed on 1 April 1992 and its sole task is the management of the Army's most precious resource, its soldiers. The Corps absorbed the functions of six existing smaller corps; the Royal Military Police, the Royal Army Pay Corps, the Royal Army Educational Corps, the Royal Army Chaplains Department, the Army Legal Corps and the Military Provost Staff Corps.

The Corps is organised into four branches, Staff and Personnel Support (SPS), Provost, Educational and Training Services (ETS) and Army Legal Services (ALS). In late 1996 the AGC consisted of over 7,190 officers and soldiers.

The Role of SPS Branch

The role of SPS Branch is to ensure the efficient and smooth delivery of Personnel Administration to the Army. This includes support to individual officers and soldiers in units by processing pay and Service documentation, first line provision of financial, welfare, education and resettlement guidance to individuals and the provision of clerical skills and information management to ensure the smooth day to day running of the unit or department.

AGC (SPS) officers are employed throughout the Army, in direct support of units as Regimental Administrative Officers or AGC Detachment Commanders. They hold Commander AGC(SPS) and SO2 AGC(SPS) posts in district/ Divisional and Brigade HQs and fill posts at the Adjutant General's Information Centre (AGIC) and general staff appointment throughout the Army headquarters locations.

AGC(SPS) soldiers are employed as Military Clerks in direct support of units within the

AGC Field Detachments, in fixed centre pay offices, in headquarters to provide staff support and in miscellaneous posts such as embassy clerks, as management accountants or in AGIC as programmer analysts.

Currently, about 62% of AGC(SPS) soldiers are based in UK, 27% in Germany and 11% elsewhere. The majority, currently 70%, are serving with field force units, with the remaining 30% in base and training units or HQs, such as MoD.

Members of AGC(SPS) are first trained as soldiers and then specialise as Military Clerks. AGC(SPS) officers complete the same military training as their counterparts in other Arms and Services, starting as the Royal Military Academy, Sandhurst. They are required to attend all promotion courses such as the Junior Command and Staff Course, and to pass the standard career exams prior to promotion to the rank of Major.

Organisation of a Regimental Administrative Office

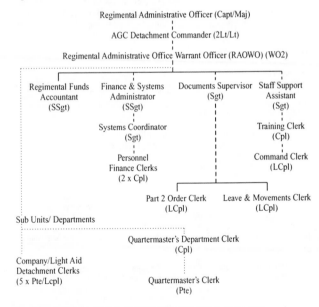

Note: Most major units will have an administrative office similar to the above.

The principal functional tasks of AGC(SPS) personnel on operations are:

a. The maintenance of Field Records, including the soldiers Record of Service, casualty reporting and disciplinary documentation.

b. Clerical and staff support to Battle Group HQs and independent Sub Units such as Engineer and Logistic Squadrons.

c. The issue of pay and allowances to personnel.

d. The maintenance of Imprest Accounts (the MoD Public Accounts) which involve paying local suppliers for services, receiving cash from non-Army agencies such as NAAFI and Forces Post Office receipts.

e. The deployment of a Field Records Cell which coordinates all personnel administration in the field.

f. AGC(SPS) personnel play a full part in operational duties by undertaking such tasks as local defence, guards and command post duties. In addition, Commanding Officers can employ any soldier in their unit as they see fit and may require AGC(SPS) personnel to undertake appropriate additional training to allow them to be used in some specialist roles specific to the unit, or as radio operators or drivers.

The Role of the Provost Branch

The Provost Branch was formed from the formerly independent Corps of Royal Military Police (RMP) and the Military Provost Staff Corps (MPSC). Although they are no longer independent they are still known as the AGC (PRO) and AGC (MPS) thus forming the two parts of the Provost Branch.

Royal Military Police

To provide the police support the Army requires the RMP has the following functions:

a. Providing operational support to units in the field.

b. Preventing crime.

c. Enforcement of the law within the community and assistance with the maintenance of discipline.

d. Providing a 24 hour response service of assistance, advice and information.

Operational support includes advising commanders and the staff who produce the operational movement plans. RMP traffic posts are deployed along the main operational movement routes and provide a constant flow of traffic information regarding the progress of front line troops and the logistical resupply. RMP with a vehicle to man ratio of 1:3 are also a valuable force for the security of rear areas. In addition there is a highly trained RMP close protection group that specialises in the protection of high risk VIPs.

The RMP provide the day to day police support for both the Army in the UK and dependents and MoD civilians overseas. RMP units are trained and equipped to deal with the most serious crimes. The Special Investigation Branch (SIB) operates in a similar fashion to the civilian CID.

The Military Provost Staff

AGC(MPS) staff are recruited from within the Army are carefully selected for the leadership, management and training skills necessary to motivate the predominantly young offenders with whom they work. The majority of AGC(MPS) personnel are located in the Military Corrective Training Centre (MCTC) at Colchester where offenders sentenced by military courts are confined.

The Role of the ETS Branch

The AGC(ETS) Branch has the responsibility of improving the efficiency, effectiveness and morale of the Army by providing support to operations and the developmental education, training, support and resettlement services that the Army requires to carry out its task. ETS personnel provide assistance at almost all levels of command but their most visible task is the manning of Army Education Centres wherever the Army is stationed. At these centres officers and soldiers receive the educational support necessary for them to achieve both civilian and military qualifications.

The Role of the ALS Branch

The AGC(ALS) Branch advises on all aspects of service and civilian law that may affect every level of the Army from General to Private soldiers. Members of the branch are usually qualified as solicitors or barristers. In addition to the AGC personnel attached to major units throughout the Army the Corps is directly responsible for the following:

Smaller Corps

THE INTELLIGENCE CORPS (Int Corps) - The Int Corps deals with operational intelligence, counter intelligence and security.

THE ROYAL ARMY VETERINARY CORPS (RAVC) - The RAVC looks after the many animals that the Army has on strength. Veterinary tasks in today's Army are mainly directed towards guard or search dogs and horses for ceremonial duties.

THE ARMY PHYSICAL TRAINING CORPS (APTC) - Consists mainly of SNCOs who are responsible for unit fitness. The majority of major units have a representative from this corps on their strength.

THE GENERAL SERVICE CORPS (GSC) - A holding unit for specialists. Personnel from this corps are generally members of the Reserve Army.

SMALL ARMS SCHOOL CORPS (SASC) A small corps with the responsibility of training instructors in all aspects of weapon handling.

CHAPTER 11 - UNITS OF THE REGULAR ARMY

The Cavalry

After the re-organisation following the Options for Change review, consists of 11 armoured regiments and one mounted ceremonial regiment as follows:

The Household Cavalry

The Household Cavalry Regiment	HCR
The Household Cavalry Mounted Regiment	HCMR

The Royal Armoured Corps

1st The Queen's Dragoon Guards	QDG
The Royal Scots Dragoon Guards	SCOTS DG
The Royal Dragoon Guards	RDG
The Queen's Royal Hussars	QRH
9th/12th Royal Lancers	9/12L
The King's Royal Hussars	KRH
The Light Dragoons	LD
The Queen's Royal Lancers	QRL
1st Royal Tank Regiment	1 RTR
2nd Royal Tank Regiment	2 RTR

Permanent Locations:

United Kingdom	-	4 Regiments
Germany	-	7 Regiments

The Infantry

Divided into 40 general service battalions, plus six battalions of the Royal Irish Regiment which will be used only in Northern Ireland, and the Special Air Service Regiment.

The Guards Division

1st Bn Grenadier Guards	1 GREN GDS
1st Bn Coldstream Guards	1 COLM GDS
1st Bn Scots Guards	1 SG
1st Bn Irish Guards	1 IG
1st Bn Welsh Guards	1 WG

There are generally three battalions from the Guards Division on public duties in London at any one time. When a Regiment is stationed in London on public duties it is given an extra company to ensure the additional manpower required for ceremonial events is available.

The Scottish Division

1st Bn The Royal Scots	1 RS
1st Bn The Royal Highland Fusiliers	1 RHF
1st Bn The King's Own Scottish Borderers	1 KOSB
1st Bn The Black Watch	1 BW
1st Bn The Argyll & Sutherland Highlanders	1 A and SH
1st Bn The Highlanders	1 HLDRS

The Queen's Division

1st Bn The Princess of Wales's Royal Regiment (Queen's and Royal Hampshire)	1 PWRR
2nd Bn The Princess of Wales's Royal Regiment (Queen's and Royal Hampshire)	2 PWRR
1st Bn The Royal Regiment of Fusiliers	1 RRF
2nd Bn The Royal Regiment of Fusiliers	2 RRF
1st Bn The Royal Anglian Regiment	1 R ANGLIAN
2nd Bn The Royal Anglian Regiment	2 R ANGLIAN

The King's Division

1st Bn The King's Own Royal Border Regiment	1 KOBR
1st Bn The King's Regiment	1 KINGS
1st Bn The Prince of Wales's Own Regiment of Yorkshire	1 PWO
1st Bn The Green Howards	1 GH
1st Bn The Queen's Lancashire Regiment	1 QLR
1st Bn The Duke of Wellington's Regiment	1 DWR

The Prince of Wales's Division

1st Bn The Devonshire & Dorset Regiment	1 D and D
1st Bn The Cheshire Regiment	1 CHESHIRE
1st Bn The Royal Welch Fusiliers	1 RWF
1st Bn The Royal Regiment of Wales	1 RRW
1st Bn The Royal Gloucestershire, Berkshire and Wiltshire Regiment	1 RGBW
1st Bn The Worcestershire & Sherwood Foresters Regiment	1 WFR
1st Bn The Staffordshire Regiment	1 STAFFORDS

The Light Division

1st Bn The Light Infantry	1 LI
2nd Bn The Light Infantry	2 LI
1st Bn The Royal Green Jackets	1 RGJ
2nd Bn The Royal Green Jackets	2 RGJ

The Brigade of Gurkhas

1st Bn The Royal Gurkha Regiment	1 RGR
2nd Bn The Royal Gurkha Regiment	2 RGR

The Parachute Regiment

1st Bn The Parachute Regiment	1 PARA
2nd Bn The Parachute Regiment	2 PARA
3rd Bn The Parachute Regiment	3 PARA

The Royal Irish Regiment

1st Bn The Royal Irish Regiment	1 R IRISH
3rd/4th/ 5th/7th/8th/9th Royal Irish Regiment*	3-9 R IRISH

* The 3rd to 8th Bns The Royal Irish Regiment are employed exclusively in Northern Ireland and were formerly battalions of The Ulster Defence Regiment. The 4/5 Rangers is a TA Battalion stationed in Northern Ireland and wearing the Royal Irish capbadge.

Infantry Battalions - Permanent Locations

United Kingdom	-	31 Battalions
Germany	-	6 Battalions
Cyprus	-	2 Battalions
Hong Kong	-	1 Battalion (on detachment from UK until withdrawal in 1997)
Brunei	-	1 Gurkha Battalion

There are three infantry training battalions at the Infantry Training Centre located at Catterick in North Yorkshire.

The Special Air Service Regiment

The 22nd Special Air Service Regiment   22 SAS

The SAS can be classed as an infantry unit but the members of the regiment are found from all arms and services in the Army after exhaustive selection tests.

The Support Arms

The Royal Regiment of Artillery (RA)

1st Regiment Royal Horse Artillery	1 RHA	(Field)
3rd Regiment Royal Horse Artillery	3 RHA	(Field)
4th Regiment	4 REGT	(Field)
5th Regiment	5 REGT	(MLRS)
7th Regiment Royal Horse Artillery	7 RHA	(Parachute)
12th Regiment	12 REGT	(Air Defence)
14th Regiment	14 REGT	(Training)
16th Regiment	16 REGT	(Air Defence)
19th Regiment	19 REGT	(Field)
22nd Regiment	22 REGT	(Air Defence)
26th Regiment	26 REGT	(Field)
29th Commando Regiment	29 REGT	(Field)
32nd Regiment	32 REGT	(MLRS)
39th Regiment	39 REGT	(MLRS)
40th Regiment	40 REGT	(Field)
47th Regiment	47 REGT	(Air Defence)

Permanent Locations	-	at late 1996
United Kingdom	-	11 Regiments
Germany	-	5 Regiments

The Corps of Royal Engineers (RE)

1st RSME Regiment	1 RSME REGT
3rd RSME Regiment	3 RSME REGT
21st Engineer Regiment	21 ENGR REGT
22nd Engineer Regiment	22 ENGR REGT
25th Engineer Regiment	25 ENGR REGT
28th Engineer Regiment	28 ENGR REGT
32nd Engineer Regiment	32 ENGR REGT
33rd Engineer Regiment	33 ENGR REGT (EOD)
35th Engineer Regiment	35 ENGR REGT
36th Engineer Regiment	36 ENGR REGT

38th Engineer Regiment	38 ENGR REGT
39th Engineer Regiment	39 ENGR REGT

Permanent Locations

United Kingdom	-	8 Regiments
Germany	-	4 Regiments

The total for the UK includes the 2 x RSME Training Regiments.

The Royal Corps of Signals (R SIGNALS)

1st (UK) Armd Div HQ and Signal Regiment	1 SIG REGT
2nd Signal Regiment	2 SIG REGT
3rd (UK) Div HQ & Signal Regiment	3 SIG REGT
7th (ARRC) Signal Regiment	7 SIG REGT
9th Signal Regiment (Radio)	9 SIG REGT
11th Signal Regiment (Trg Regt)	11 SIG REGT
14th Signal Regiment (Electronic Warfare)	14 SIG REGT
15th Signal Regiment	15 SIG REGT
16th Signal Regiment	16 SIG REGT
21st Signal Regiment (Air Support)	21 SIG REGT
30th Signal Regiment	30 SIG REGT

Permanent Locations

United Kingdom	-	7 Regiments
Germany	-	3 Regiments
Cyprus	-	1 Regiment
Hong Kong	-	1 Regiment (until withdrawal)

The Army Air Corps (AAC)

1st Regiment	1 REGT AAC
3rd Regiment	3 REGT AAC
4th Regiment	4 REGT AAC
7th Regiment	7 REGT AAC
9th Regiment	9 REGT AAC

Permanent Locations

United Kingdom	-	4 Regiments
Germany	-	1 Regiment

THE SERVICES

The Royal Logistic Corps (RLC)

1 General Support Regiment	1 (GS)	REGT
2 Close Support Regiment	2 (CS)	REGT
3 Close Support Regiment	3 (CS)	REGT
4 General Support Regiment	4 (GS)	REGT
5 Territorial Army Training Regiment	5 (TRG)	REGT
6 Support Regiment	6 (SP)	REGT
7 Transport Regiment	7 (TPT)	REGT
8 Artillery Support Regiment	8 (ARTY SP)	REGT
9 Supply Regiment	9 (SUP)	REGT
10 Transport Regiment	10 (TPT)	REGT
11 Explosive Ordnance Disposal Regiment	11 (EOD)	REGT
12 Supply Regiment	12 (SUP)	REGT
14 Supply Regiment	14 (SUP)	REGT
17 Port and Maritime Regiment	17 (PORT)	REGT
21 Logistic Support Regiment	21 (LOG SP)	REGT
23 Pioneer Regiment	23 (PNR)	REGT
24 Regiment	24 REGT	
27 Transport Regiment	27 (TPT)	REGT
29 Regiment	29 REGT	
89 Postal and Courier Regiment	89 (PC)	REGT

Miscellaneous RLC Major Units
Training Regiment & Depot
Postal & Courier Depot
Army School of Ammunition
Cyprus Logistic Unit
3 Base Ordnance Depot

There are Combat Service Support Batallions with the Royal Marines 3 Commando Brigade, 5 Airborne Brigade, 24 Airmobile Brigade and the AMF(L) group.

RLC major units in Germany include:

1 General Support Regiment	-	Gutersloh
2 Close Support Regiment	-	Gutersloh
6 Support Regiment	-	Gutersloh
7 Transport Regiment	-	Bielefeld
12 Supply Regiment	-	Wulfen
14 Supply Regiment	-	Dulmen
24 Regiment	-	Bielefeld

Royal Army Medical Corps (RAMC)

Has the following Regular Army field medical units:

1 Armoured Field Ambulance	1 ARMD FD AMB
2 Armoured Field Ambulance	2 ARMD FD AMB
3 Armoured Field Ambulance	3 ARMD FD AMB
16 Armoured Field Ambulance	16 ARMD FD AMB
24 Armoured Field Ambulance	24 ARMD FD AMB
4 Field Ambulance	4 FD AMB
5 Field Ambulance	5 FD AMB
19 Airmobile Field Ambulance	19 AIRMOB FD AMB
23 Parachute Field Ambulance	23 PARA FD AMB
21 Field Hospital	21 FD HOSP
33 Field Hosptal	23 FD HOSP
34 Field Hospital	34 FD HOSP
84 Field Medical Equipment Depot	84 FMED

Military Bands

Following the 1993 reorganisation of military bands on 1 Dec 1996 the Regular Army has 30 bands as follows:

Household Cavalry	- 70 musicians	-	2 bands
Grenadier Guards	- 49 musicians	-	1 band
Coldstream Guards	- 49 musicians	-	1 band
Scots Guards	- 49 musicians	-	1 band
Welsh Guards	- 49 musicians	-	1 band
Irish Guards	- 49 musicians	-	1 band
Royal Artillery	- 49 musicians	-	1 band
Royal Engineers	- 35 musicians	-	1 band
Royal Signals	- 35 musicians	-	1 band
Royal Logistic Corps	- 35 musicians	-	1 band
REME	- 35 musicians	-	1 band
Adjutant General's Corps	- 35 musicians	-	1 band
Army Air Corps	- 35 musicians	-	1 band
Royal Armoured Corps	- 140 musicians	-	4 bands
Scottish Division	- 70 musicians	-	2 bands
Queens Division	- 70 musicians	-	2 bands
Kings Division	- 70 musicians	-	2 bands
Prince of Wales's Division	- 70 musicians	-	2 bands
Light Division	- 49 musicians	-	1 band
Parachute Regiment	- 35 musicians	-	1 band
Royal Irish Regiment	- 35 musicians	-	1 band
Royal Gurkha Rifles	- 35 musicians	-	1 band

There are another 24 bands in the Territorial Army.

CHAPTER 12 - RECRUITING, SELECTION AND TRAINING

> *"If any gentlemen, soldiers or others have a mind to serve Her Majesty, and pull down the French king; if any prentices have severe masters, any children have undutiful parents; if any servants have too little wages, or any husband too much wife, let him repair to the noble Sergeant Kite, at the sign of the Raven in the good old town of Shrewsbury..."*

> Sergeant Kite 1704

Recruiting

Recruiting can best be described as the steps taken to attract sufficient men and women of the right quality to meet the Army's personnel requirements. Selection is the process that is carried out to ensure that those who are accepted into the Army have the potential to be good soldiers and are capable of being trained to carry out their chosen trade. Training is the process of preparing those men and women for their careers in the Army. Training is progressive and continues all the way through a soldier's career.

The Director General Army Manning and Recruiting (DGAMR), a Major General in The Ministry of Defence, is responsible for ensuring that the Army is properly manned and that sufficient men and women of the right quality are recruited to meet the needs of the service.

An MOD committee called the Standing Committee Army Manpower Forecasts (SCAMF) calculates the numbers that need to be enlisted to maintain the Army's personnel at the correct level. The Committee needs to take account of changing unit establishments, wastage caused by servicemen and women leaving the service at the end of their engagements, and those who might choose to leave before their engagements come to an end (PVR - Premature Voluntary Release). The number required in each trade in the Army is assessed and figures are published at six monthly intervals so that adjustments may be made during the year.

The Director of Army Recruiting (DAR), a Brigadier in The Ministry of Defence, and his staff located throughout the United Kingdom are then responsible for the recruiting and selection to meet the personnel targets.

Potential recruits are attracted into the Army in a number of ways including advertisements on the television, in cinemas and in the press. Permanently established recruiting teams from many Regiments and Corps tour the country and staff from the Army Career Information Offices (ACIOs) visit schools, youth clubs and job centres. Young, recently trained soldiers are also sent back to their home towns and schools to talk to their friends about life in the Army and are regularly interviewed by the local press.

During 1995-96 the total cost of recruiting for all three services was £100 million and of this total the Army figure was £55 million. The approximate cost of recruits to each service was as follows:

Army	-	£5,000 per recruit
Royal Navy	-	£8,000 per recruit
Royal Air Force	-	£9,500 per recruit

Annual Army recruiting figures during the recent past are as follows:

	1992/93	1993/94	1994/95	1995/96
Officers	1,064	752	823	891
Soldiers	10,323	8,824	9,861	12,020

The 1996/97 recruiting target for soldier recruits is 15,100. However, the realistic achievement total is probably in the region of 10,500.

Soldier Selection

Potential recruits are normally aged between 16 years and 6 months and 25 years, except when they are applying for a vacancy as an apprentice when the age limits are from 15 years 8 months to 17 years 6 months.

Under the latest selection system a potential recruit will have a preliminary assessment at the ACIO. Here he or she will take the computer based Army Entrance Test (AET) which is designed to assess ability to assimilate the training required for the candidate's chosen trade. The staff at the ACIO will conduct a number of interviews to decide on overall suitability for the Army. The ACIO staff will look at references from school or any employers and offer advice on which trade may be available and might suit the candidate. A preliminary medical examination will also be carried out that checks on weight, eyesight and hearing.

If these test and interviews are successfully passed the candidate will be booked for further tests at the Recruit Selection Centre which is closest to his or her home. Recruit selection centres are at Glencorse in Scotland, Lichfield in Staffordshire, Pirbright in Surrey and Ballymena in Northern Ireland.

The candidates will remain at the RSC for an overnight stay and undergo another medical examination, a physical assessment test and an interview with a Personnel Selection Officer. The potential recruits will also see at first hand the type of training that they will undergo and the sort of life that they will lead in barracks if successful in getting into the Army. Physical fitness is assessed on a timed run and some gymnasium exercises. After further interviews the candidate is informed if he or she is successful and if so is offered a vacancy in a particular trade and Regiment or Corps.

Phase 1 Training

Basic Recruit or Phase 1 training is the same for all soldiers whatever Regiment or Corps and whichever trade they are enlisted into. The course lasts for 10 weeks and is called The Common Military Syllabus (Recruit) (CMSR). It includes training in the basic military skills required of all soldiers and incorporates Weapon Handling and Shooting, Drill, Physical Fitness, Field Tactics, Map Reading, Survival in Nuclear Chemical and Biological Warfare and General Military Knowledge. It is an intensive course and requires the recruit to show considerable determination and courage to succeed.

The Army training organisation carries out centralised Phase 1 Training at 5 Army Training Regiments (ATRs). Each ATR is responsible for training all recruits enlisting into the following Regiments and Corps (with the exception of apprentices).

ATR Pirbright - The Household Cavalry, Infantry of the Guards Division, The Royal Logistic Corps, the Royal Electrical and Mechanical Engineers and the Royal Artillery.

ATR Bassingbourne - The Royal Engineers, The Royal Signals and Infantry of the Queen's Division.

ATR Winchester - The Royal Armoured Corps, Infantry of the Light Division, The Army Air Corps, The Adjutant General's Corps (including the Royal Military Police) and The Intelligence Corps.

ATR Glencorse - Infantry of the Scottish and King's Divisions.

ATR Lichfield - Infantry of the Prince of Wales Division, The Parachute Regiment, Royal Army Medical Corps, Royal Army Veterinary Corps, Royal Army Dental Corps and Queen Alexandra's Royal Army Nursing Corps.

Phase 1 Training for the Royal Irish Regiment takes place at Ballymena in Northern Ireland.

Gurkha recruits are now trained at Church Crookham following the closure of the Training Depot Brigade of Gurkhas in Hong Kong. The first intake of 153 men selected from 57,000 applicants started training in the UK during 1995.

Phase 2 Training

Phase 2 training is the 'Special to Arm' training that is required to prepare soldiers who have recently completed their basic Phase 1 training, to enable them to take their place in field force units of their Regiment or Corps. This phase of training has no fixed period and courses vary considerably in length.

As an example infantry Phase 2 training is reported to take 11 weeks.

Phase 2 training for the major Arms and Services is carried out as follows:

The Royal Armoured Corps - Takes place at Bovington Camp in Dorset. Recruits into the Household Cavalry Regiment also undergo equitation training.

Infantry - Infantry recruits do their 12 week Phase 2 Training at the Infantry Training Battalion in Catterick.

The Royal Artillery - At the Royal School of Artillery at Larkhill in Wiltshire.

The Royal Engineers - At Cove in Hampshire and at the Royal School of Military Engineering at Chatham in Kent.

The Royal Logistic Corps Drivers are trained at Leconfield, supply specialists at Blackdown, Cooks at Aldershot and Pioneers at Northampton.

The Adjutant General's Corps - Pay and Clerks are trained at the AGC Depot at Worthy Down near Winchester and the Royal Militay Police at Chichester.

Royal Electrical and Mechanical Engineers - Vehicle Mechanics are trained at Bordon and other trades at Arborfield.

Royal Signals - Training takes place at the Royal School of Signals at Blandford in Dorset.

Royal Army Medical Corps - At the RAMC Depot at Keogh Barracks, Aldershot. Apprentices Phase 1 and Phase 2 training which can last for up to two years is conducted at the Army Apprentice College. On entry Apprentices are generally aged between 16 years and 17 years and 6 months.

Commissions

There are two main types of commission in the Army. These are:

a. THE REGULAR COMMISSION (Reg C) which is for those who wish to make the Army their permanent career. Regular Officers can normally expect their career to last until their 55th birthday.

b. THE SHORT SERVICE COMMISSION (SSC) which is for those who remain uncertain about their long-term career plans. The SSC lasts for a minimum of 3 years (6 for the Army Air Corps) but can be extended if mutually agreed to a maximum of 8 years.

The minimum educational requirements for a Regular Officer are currently 5 passes at GCSE which must include English Language, Mathematics and either a Science subject or Modern Language. Two of the passes must be at 'A' level grades A to E. Some Corps only accept candidates with appropriate degrees or professional qualifications.

The requirements for a Short Service Commission are less stringent requiring only 5 passes at GCSE grades A-C including English Language or Mathematics. Candidates for commissions should be over 17 years and 9 months and under 25 years old when they begin officer training.

c. SHORT SERVICE LIMITED COMMISSION - The SSLC is a commission that is aimed at those who have completed their 'A' Levels and have a gap year prior to entering University. The selection procedure at RCB has to be completed after which a three week course at Sandhurst is attended. Those who successfully complete the course join their chosen Regiment or Corps as 2nd Lieutenants for a minimum of 4 months and a maximum of 18 months with a front-line unit, but not on active service. The purpose of the SSLC is to create a pool of young men and women who will take a favourable impression of the Army into their careers.

d. LATE ENTRY COMMISSIONS - A number of vacancies exist for senior Non Commissioned Officers and Warrant Officers to be granted commissions known as Late Entry Commissions. Officers commissioned from the ranks are initially employed in exactly the same way as those granted direct entry commissions but because of their age, generally do not rise above the rank of Major.

Officer Selection & Sandhurst

Candidates for commissions are normally advised by a Schools or University Liaison Officer of the options open to them and it is he who arranges interviews and familiarisation visits to an appropriate Regiment or Corps. If the Regiment or Corps is prepared to sponsor a candidate, they then guide him or her through the rest of the selection procedure. All candidates are required to attend the Regular Commissions Board (RCB) at Westbury, Wiltshire for a three day assessment prior to which they should have undergone a medical examination and attended a pre-RCB briefing so that they know what to expect.

RCB consists of a series of interviews and tests that assess the personality and the leadership potential in applicants. There is no secret in the selection procedures and details are available for all applicants.

RCB may, in some cases, require further development in either leadership skills or academic standards prior to beginning officer training and this is conducted on a 12 week course at Rowallan Company at The Royal Military Academy Sandhurst (RMAS) which is at Camberley in Surrey.

All potential officers accepted for training attend the RMAS Common Commissioning Course which lasts for 44 weeks with 3 entries a year in January, May and September. After successfully completing the Sandhurst course a young officer then completes a further specialist course with his or her chosen Regiment or Corps.

Females cannot be accepted in the Household Cavalry, The Royal Armoured Corps or the Infantry. Also some other Regiments and Corps restrict the number of vacancies open to women.

Welbeck College

Welbeck is the Army's sixth form college which offers two year 'A' Level courses for boys and girls who wish to gain commissions in the technical Corps. The Welbeck course is science and engineering based and includes leadership training, Welbexians do not need to attend the Regular Commissions Board but simply require the recommendation of the Headmaster to gain entry to RMAS.

Army Training Overview

Responsible for Army Training is the Inspectorate General of Doctrine and Training (IGDT) based at Upavon in Wiltshire. It employs about 18,000 service and civilian personnel (the majority in the UK and Germany) with a budget of over £500 million annually. HQ IGDT has 103 military staff and 116 civilian personnel and is directly responsible to the Adjutant General.

Following basic Phase 1 and Phase 2 training, soldiers are posted to their units and progressive training is carried out on a continual basis. Training is geared to individual, sub-unit or formation level and units regularly train outside of the UK and Germany. As would be expected, there are specialist unit training packages for specific operational commitments such as Northern Ireland and Yugoslavia.

For example, the training package for personnel warned off for deployment to the former Yugoslavia consists of a 12 day special-to-mission package. The training is carried out by specialist training advisory teams at the Army's Combined Arms Training Centre at Warminster and for Germany based units, at the Sennelager Training Centre.

The British Army's main training areas outside of Europe are:

Canada - Suffield

British Army Training Unit Suffield (BATUS) has the responsibility to train battlegroups in the planning and execution of armoured operations through the medium of live firing and tactical test exercise. There are 6 x Medicine Man battlegroup exercises each year in a training season that lasts from March to November.

Canada - Wainright

The British Army Training Support Unit at Wainright (BATSU(W)) provides the logistic and administrative support for Infantry units at the Canadian Forces training base in Western Canada. During the winter months the unit moves in its entirety to Fort Lewis in the USA where it carries out a similar function. There are usually 3 battalion group exercises at Wainright and 2 at Fort Lewis during the course of each training year.

Kenya

British Army Liaison Staff Kenya (BATLSK) is responsible for supporting Infantry battlion group exercises and approximately 3,000 British troops train in Kenya each year in a harsh unforgiving terrain, ranging in altitude from 8,000 feet down to 2,300 feet. BATLSK has been based at its present site in Kahawa Barracks since Kenya's independence in 1963.

Belize

The British Army Training Support unit Belize (BATSUB) was formed on 1 October 1994. Its role is to give training and logistic support to Land Command units training in a tropical jungle environment. During its first full year of operation BATSUB cost £3.1 million.

Overseas Students

During the 1993-1994 financial year, 4,566 students from 98 different countries took part in training in the United Kingdom. The charges for training depend on the length of the course, its syllabus and the numbers taking part. Receipts from overseas governments for this training are believed to be in the region of £39,500,000. There are only 166 countries that actually have armed forces. Figures for 1996/97 are likely to be similar.

Training Standards

Shooting: - All ranks are required to take an annual personnel weapons test (APWT). Pass rates for 1992/93 (the latest year for which figures are available) were:

Infantry	-	98%
Royal Armoured Corps	-	85%
Royal Engineers	-	74%
Royal Artillery	-	78%
Royal Signals	-	88%
Royal Logistic Corps	-	89%
Army Average	-	86%

Basic Fitness Test: All soldiers of all ranks and ages are required to take a basic fitness test. This test involves a 1.5 mile run and walk (in a squad) on level ground and in training shoes, in 10 minutes for those under 30. There are gradually rising time limits for older personnel and recruits in training are given 10 mins and 30 seconds for the 1.5 mile run. The current standards for women are lower and female recruits are allowed to do the 1.5 mile run in 12 minutes and 50 seconds.

Recruit Training Assessments - During Recruit Training personnel are assessed at different stages of training as follows:

Test	Introduction	Interim	Final
Heaves	2	4	6
Sit Up Test	1 Min (20 reps)	2 min (42 reps)	3 min (65 reps)
1.5 Mile Run	11 min 30 sec	11 mins	10 min 30 sec

148

Career Profile - Soldier

As an illustration of the career that might be expected for a regular soldier, we have used a model based on the career of Thomas Atkins, a serving soldier about to retire after 22 years' service.

Age

17 - Left school at 16. Bored with life at home and not happy in his job with British Rail. Decides to join the Army, and takes selection tests at his local Army Careers Office. After a successful assessment at the Recruit Selection Centre he is sent to an Army Training Regiment to complete Phase1 Common Military Syllabus (Recruit) Training lasting ten weeks. Following completion of the course he attends the Infantry Training Centre at Catterick for a further 12 week course where the specialist infantry skills are taught. After initial training Atkins is posted to a regular battalion of his regiment which is serving in Cyprus. Spends 18 months in Cyprus where he is employed as a rifleman in an infantry platoon.

19 - The battalion is posted to Tidworth in Hampshire. Rfn Atkins is transferred from an infantry platoon in A Company to the Anti-Tank Platoon in Support Company. Atkins sees this move as a career advancement, and from Tidworth completes a 6-month tour in Ulster. About two and a half years after arriving in Tidworth the battalion is posted to Belfast on an 18-month tour.

21 - Directly after the move to Belfast Rfn Atkins attends a battalion NCOs training course and is promoted to Lcpl. As a Lcpl he is the 2ic of an infantry section in a rifle platoon operating in some of the most dangerous parts of the city. After a year in Belfast, he is promoted to Cpl and attends a Weapons Instructors Course lasting 8 weeks at the School of Infantry in Wiltshire.

23 - The battalion leaves Belfast on posting to Germany as an armoured infantry battalion mounted in Warrior armoured fighting vehicles. Cpl Atkins is posted to the Army Training Regiment where he is responsible for training a section of recruits. After two years at the Army Training Regiment he rejoins his battalion that still has two years of its four year tour left to serve.

25 - Spends one year in Germany commanding an infantry section mounted in a Warrior AIFV during which time the battalion spends six months on operations in support of NATO forces in Bosnia. At the end of this year attends a Platoon Sergeants Course at the School of Infantry, and on rejoining the battalion after the course is promoted Sergeant.

26 - Becomes 2ic of a rifle platoon, is responsible for the on the job training of a young officer and the welfare of the 35 soldiers in his care.

On occasions, he commands the platoon in the absence of the officer platoon commander.

30 - Promoted to Colour Sergeant and becomes an instructor at the Royal Military Academy Sandhurst where he teaches officer cadets some of the fundamentals of soldiering. After Sandhurst, returns to the battalion now serving in Cyprus where he runs the logistical support for an infantry company.

33 - Promoted WOII (Company Sergeant Major) and is almost entirely responsible for the discipline and administration of an infantry company of about 130 men.

36 Appointed RQMS (Regimental Quartermaster Sergeant) and is now responsible for much of the logistic support for a complete infantry battalion.

38 - Promoted WOI (Regimental Sergeant Major). The most senior soldier in the battalion and very much the Commanding Officer's right hand man. Much feared by the scruffy and the idle, avoided by young officers with long hair, the reputation of the battalion is his personal responsibility.

40 At the end of his service leaves the Army and returns to civilian life.

Note: Not all RSM's return to civilian life at the end of 22 years service. Many are offered commissions and fill important posts in both regiments and corps, often as Quartermasters responsible for equipment worth many millions of pounds. For example the Quartermaster of a cavalry regiment may be responsible for tanks, armoured vehicles and associated items on charge to the regiment worth some £250 million. As long ago as the First World War, Field Marshal Sir William Robertson (a commissioned warrant officer) became Chief of the Imperial General Staff.

Career Profile - Officer

To illustrate an officer's career, we have used a non graduate regular officer who has elected to serve in the infantry.

Age

19 - Having left school with 2 A Levels decides to join the Army and goes to the Regular Commissions Board (RCB) at Westbury in Wiltshire to undergo selection. On being passed by the RCB as a suitable candidate for a commission, is given a date to start at the Royal Military Academy, Sandhurst (RMA). At the RMA he completes a one year course, designed to give young officers a sound basic military education. Following graduation from Sandhurst he attends the 12 week Platoon Commanders Battle Course at the School of Infantry.

20 - Posted to a battalion of his Regiment as a 2/Lt. The battalion is serving in Catterick and he commands a rifle platoon for two years. During his tour as a platoon commander the battalion serves in South Armagh on a six month tour and takes part in an exercise in Kenya. After two years is promoted to Lt.

22 - Posted to the Infantry Training Centre where he commands a number of Training Platoons during a two year posting. Training Platoons usually have experienced regular NCOs as instructors and their task is to take soldiers from the Army Training Regiments and turn them into infantrymen during a 12 week course.

24 - Returns to the battalion and commands the Mortar Platoon for a further 18 months, having undergone a conversion course at the School of Infantry. During this time he is detached from the battalion for 4 months and works as a junior staff officer in Bosnia. At the end of this period is selected to become the Battalion Adjutant and is responsible for the day-today discipline and administration of the battalion.

27 - On appointment as Adjutant he is promoted Captain.

29 - After two years as Adjutant he is posted away from the battalion, and spends the next two years as an infantry exchange officer in the United States.

31 - Returns to the battalion now serving in Germany and becomes the 2i/c of an armoured infantry company. During this time he starts to prepare himself for an examination which if he passes will qualify him for promotion to Major, and if he does extremely well, will qualify for a place at the Staff College.

32 - Becomes the Battalion Operations Officer, responsible to the Commanding Officer for preparing the battalion's war plans. Passes the Staff/ Promotion exam and is given a place at the Staff College.

33 - Attends a course at the Staff College Camberley. After one year at the Staff College is promoted to major and posted to HQ 5th Division as a staff officer in the Operations Branch (SO2 G3)

36 - Returns to the battalion now serving in Tidworth where he commands a mechanised rifle company (mounted in Saxon APCs) for two years. During this period the battalion serves on a six month tour in support of the UN in Bosnia.

38 - Posted to HQ 1(UK) Armoured Division where he fills a staff officer's post in the Training Branch.

39 - Selected for promotion to Lt Col and returns to the battalion once again serving in Germany. He now commands a Battlegroup composed of tanks, infantry, artillery and engineers.

42 - Promoted to Colonel and becomes a staff officer at PJHQ Northwood working for the Director of Joint Operations.

47 - Is promoted to Brigadier and commands an Armoured Brigade in Germany.

50 - Commands a Division in the Allied Rapid Reaction Corps (ARRC) as a Major General.

55 - Retires as a Lieutenant General to become a television personality. Is constantly seen on BBC Newsnight commenting on newsworthy crisis situations. Finally ends up as the Inspector of HM Prisons and constantly makes headlines while trying to improve standards.

CHAPTER 13 RESERVE FORCES

Strength of Territorial Army (1 January 1997)

Armour	7 Regiments*
Royal Artillery	6 Regiments
Royal Engineers	9 Regiments
Infantry	36 Battalions
Special Air Service	2 Regiments
Signals	11 Regiments
Equipment Support	5 Battalions
Logistics	11 Regiments
Equipment Support	5 Battalions
Medical	18 Hospitals/Field Ambulances

* One is an armoured reconnaissance regiment and the remainder national defence reconnaissance regiments.

Territorial Army Order of Battle:

Royal Armoured Corps
Royal Yeomanry
Royal Wessex Yeomanry
Royal Mercian and Lancastrian Yeomanry
Queen's Own Scottish Yeomanry
The King's Own Yorkshire Yeomanry (Light Infantry)
North Irish Horse

Infantry

Scottish Division
The Lowland Volunteers
3rd (Volunteer) Battalion The Royal Highland Fusiliers (Princess Margaret's Own Glasgow and Ayrshire Regiment)
3rd (Volunteer) Battalion The Black Watch (The Royal Highland Regiment)
3rd (Volunteer) Battalion The Highlanders (Seaforths, Gordons and Camerons)
7/8th (Volunteer) Battalion The Argyll and Sutherland Highlanders (Princess Louise's)

Queen's Division
5th (Volunteer) Battalion The Princess of Wales's Royal Regiment
6/7th (Volunteer) Battalion Princess of Wales's Royal Regiment
The London Regiment
5th (Volunteer) Battalion The Royal Regiment of Fusiliers
6th Northumberland Battalion The Royal Regiment of Fusiliers
6th (Volunteer) Battalion The Royal Anglian Regiment

7th (Volunteer) Battalion The Royal Anglian Regiment

King's Division
4th (Volunteer) Battalion The King's Own Royal Border Regient
5/8th (Volunteer) Battalion The King's Regiment
3rd (Volunteer) Battalion The Prince of Wales's Own Regiment of Yorkshire
4/5th Battalion The Green Howards (Alexandra Princess of Wales's Own Yorkshire
Regiment)(Yorkshire Volunteers)
4th (Volunteer) Battalion The Queen's Lancashire Regiment
3rd (Volunteer) Battalion The Duke of Wellington's Regiment (West Riding)

The Prince of Wales's Division
4th (Volunteer) Battalion The Devonshire and Dorset Regiment
3rd (Volunteer) Battalion The Cheshire Regiment
3rd (Volunteer) Battalion The Royal Welch Fusiliers
3rd (Volunteer) Battalion The Royal Regiment of Wales (24/41st Foot)
2nd (Volunteer) Battalion The Royal Gloucester, Berkshire and Wiltshire Regiment
3rd (Volunteer) Battalion The Worcestershire and Sherwood Foresters Regiment
(29th/45th Foot)
3rd (Volunteer) Battalion The Staffordshire Regiment (The Prince of Wales's)

The Light Division
5th Battalion The Light Infantry (V)
6th Battalion The Light Infantry (V)
7th Battalion The (Durham) Light Infantry (V)
4th (V) Battalion The Royal Green Jackets
5th (V) Battalion The Royal Green Jackets

The Royal Irish Regiment
4/5th (Volunteer) Battalion The Royal Irish Rangers

The Parachute Regiment
4th (Volunteer) Battalion The Parachute Regiment
10th (Volunteer) Battalion The Parachute Regiment

Special Air Service Regiment
21st Special Air Service Regiment (Artists) (V)
23rd Special Air Service Regiment (V)

Royal Regiment of Artillery
Honourable Artillery Company
100 Regiment Royal Artillery (V)
100 (Yeomanry) Regiment Royal Artillery (V)
101 Regiment Royal Artillery (V)
103 (Lancashire Artillery Volunteers) Regiment Royal Artillery
104 Regiment Royal Artillery (V)

105 Regiment Royal Artillery (V)
266 (Gloucester Volunteer Artillery) Battery Royal Horse Artillery
All Arms Watchkeeper and Liaison Officer Pool
Royal Artillery Specialist Pool (V)

Corps of Royal Engineers
Royal Monmouthshire Royal Engineers (Militia)
71 Engineer Regiment Royal Engineers (V)
72 Engineer Regiment Royal Engineers (V)
72 (Tyne Electrical Engineers) Regiments (V)
73 Engineer Regiment Royal Engineers (V)
76 Engineer Regiment Royal Engineers (V)
77 Engineer Regiment Royal Engineers (V) (Airfield Damage Repair)
78 Engineer Regiment Royal Engineers (V)
101 Engineer Regiment Royal Engineers (V) (Explosive Ordnance Disposal)
74 Field Squadron Royal Engineers (V)
131 Independent Commando Squadron Royal Engineers (V)
135 Independent Topographic Squadron Royal Engineers (V)
Jersey Field Squadron Royal Engineers (V)
198 Field Park Squadron Royal Engineers (V)
412 Amphibious Engineer Troop Royal Engineers (V)
501 Specialist Team Royal Engineers (Bulk Petroleum) (V)
502 Specialist Team Royal Engineers (Bulk Petroleum) (V)
503 Specialist Team Royal Engineers (Bulk Petroleum) (V)
504 Specialist Team Royal Engineers (Works) (V)
505 Specialist Team Royal Engineers (Bulk Petroleum) (V)
506 Specialist Team Royal Engineers (Railway Construction) (V)
507 Specialist Team Royal Engineers (Railway Construction) (V)
508 Specialist Team Royal Engineers (Works) (V)
509 Specialist Team Royal Engineers (Construction) (V)
510 Specialist Team Royal Engineers (Construction) (V)
511 Specialist Team Royal Engineers (Construction) (V)
513 Specialist Team Royal Engineers (Construction) (V)
514 Specialist Team Royal Engineers (Construction) (V)
515 Specialist Team Royal Engineers (Construction) (V)
517 Specialist Team Royal Engineers (Construction) (V)
518 Specialist Team Royal Engineers (Construction) (V)
520 Specialist Team Royal Engineers (Well Drilling) (V)
525 Specialist Team Royal Engineers (Works) (V)
526 Specialist Team Royal Engineers (Works) (V)
528 Specialist Team Royal Engineers (Construction) (V)
Engineer and Transport Staff Corps (V)
Royal Engineers Specialist Advisory Team (V)

Royal Corps of Signals
31 Greater London Signal Regiment (V)

32 Scottish Signal Regiment (V)
33 (London and Cheshire) Signal Regiment (V)
34 (Northern) Signal Regiment (V)
35 Signal Regiment (V)
36 Signal Regiment (V)
37 Signal Regiment (V)
38 Signal Regiment (V)
39 Signal Regiment (V)
40 (Ulster) Signal Regiment (V)
71 Signal Regiment (V)
1 (Special Communications) Signal Squadron (V)
2 Signal Squadron (V)
55 Independent Signal Squadron (V)
63 (Special Air Service) Signal Squadron (V)
81 Signal Squadron (V)
94 Signal Squadron (V) Intercept Troop (V)
237 Signal Squadron Reserve Troop (V)
264 (Special Air Service) Signal Squadron (V)

Army Air Corps
7 Regiment Army Air Corps (V)

Royal Army Chaplains' Department
Pool of Chaplains - Royal Army Chaplains' Department (V)

Royal Logistic Corps
Headquarters 1 Postal and Courier Group RLC (V)
85 Postal and Courier Regiment RLC (V)
86 Postal and Courier Regiment RLC (V)
87 Postal and Courier Regiment RLC (V)
150 (Northumbrian) Transport Regiment RLC (V)
151 (Greater London) Transport Regiment RLC (V)
152 (Ulster) Ambulance Transport Regiment RLC (V)
Scottish Transport Regiment RLC (V)
156 (Liverpool) Transport Regiment RLC (V)
157 (Wales) Transport Regiment RLC (V)
158 (Royal Anglian) Transport Regiment RLC (V)
160 Transport Regiment RLC (V)
164 Transport Regiment RLC (V)
161 Ambulance Regiment RLC (V)
162 Movement Control Regiment RLC (V)
163 Movement Control Regiment RLC (V)
168 Pioneer Regiment RLC (V)
165 Port Regiment RLC (V)
65 Petroleum Squadron RLC (V)
67 Middle Stores Squadron RLC (V)

68 Vehicle Squadron RLC (V)
123 Ammunition Squadron RLC (V)
124 Petroleum Squadron RLC (V)
125 Ration Squadron RLC (V)
126 Petroleum Squadron RLC (V)
142 Vehicle Squadron RLC (V)
143 Transit Squadron RLC (V)
166 Logistic Support Regiment (V)
216 (Tyne Tees) Artillery Support Squadron RLC (V
Transport Squadron RLC (V)
275 Railway Squadron RLC (V)
280 Movement Control Squadron RLC (V)
281 Movement Control Squadron RLC (V)
531 Explosive Ordnance Disposal Squadron RLC (V)
631 Explosive Ordnance Disposal Squadron RLC (V)
731 Explosive Ordnance Disposal Squadron RLC (V)
209 Printing Troop RLC (V)
383 Commando Petroleum Troop RLC (V)
395 Air Despatch Troop RLC (V)
711 Laundry Troop RLC (V)
712 Laundry Troop RLC (V)
713 Laundry Troop RLC (V)
714 Laundry Troop RLC (V)
715 Laundry Troop RLC (V)
716 Laundry Troop RLC (V)
Catering Regiment RLC (V)
Expedition Forces Institute RLC (V)

Royal Army Medical Corps
201 (Northern) Field Hospital
202 Field Hospital
203 Field Hospital
204 Field Hospital
205 Field Hospital
207 Field Hospital
208 Field Hospital
212 Field Hospital
243 (Wessex) Field Hospital
256 Field Hospital
306 Field Hospital
220 Field Ambulance
222 Field Ambulance
225 Field Ambulance
250 Field Ambulance
251 (Sunderland) Field Ambulance
253 Field Ambulance

254 Field Ambulance
Ambulance Train Squadron
144 Parachute Squadron
350 Field Surgical Team
351 Field Surgical Team
352 Field Surgical Team
353 Field Surgical Team
354 Field Surgical Team
355 Field Surgical Team
356 Field Surgical Team
357 Field Surgical Team
358 Field Surgical Team
359 Airmobile Field Surgical Team
365 Burns Specialist Team
381 Field Medical Equipment Depot
374 Head and Neck Specialist Team

Corps of Royal Electrical and Mechanical Engineers
101 Equipment Support Battalion REME (V)
102 Equipment Support Battalion REME (V)
103 Equipment Support Battalion REME (V)
104 Equipment Support Battalion REME (V)
105 Equipment Support Battalion REME (V)
Royal Electrical and Mechanical Engineers Territorial Army Officers Pool

Adjutant General's Corps (Royal Military Police)
Military Police Battalion Headquarters
116 Provost Company Royal Military Police (V)
152 Provost Company Royal Military Police (V)
163 Provost Company Royal Military Police (V)
164 Provost Company Royal Military Police (V)
165 Provost Company Royal Military Police (V)
243 Provost Company Royal Military Police (V)
251 Provost Company Royal Military Police (V)
252 Provost Company Royal Military Police (V)
253 Provost Copany Royal Military Police (V)
254 Provost Company Royal Military Police (V)
83 Section Special Investigation Branch Royal Military Police (V)

Adjutant General's Corps (Staff and Personnel Support)
Adjutant General's Corps Pool (V)

Royal Army Veterinary Corps
Royal Army Veterinary Corps Territorial Army Officers Pool

Intelligence Corps

Headquarters Intelligence and Security Group (V)
5 Communications Company (V)
20 Security Company Intelligence Corps (V)
21 Intelligence Company Intelligence Corps (V)
22 Intelligence Company Intelligence Corps (V)
23 Intelligence and Security Company Intelligence Corps (V)
24 Intelligence Company Intelligence Corps (V)
25 Intelligence and Security Company (V)
29 Security Company (V)
Technical Intelligence Staff Officers' Pool (V)

Officer Training Corps

Aberdeen University Officer Training Corps
Birmingham University Officer Training Corps
Bristol University Officer Training Corps
Cambridge University Officer Training Corps
East Midlands University Officer Training Corps
City of Edinburgh University Officer Training Corps
Exeter University Officer Training Corps
Glasgow and Strathclyde Universities Officer Training Corps
Leeds University Officer Training Corps
Liverpool University Officer Training Corps
London University Officer Training Corps
Manchester and Salford University Officer Training Corps
Northumbrian University Officer Training Corps
Oxford University Officer Training Corps
Queens University Officer Training Corps
Sheffield University Officer Training Corps
Southampton University Officer Training Corps
Tayforth University Officer Training Corps
University of Wales Officer Training Corps

Bands

Royal Yeomanry Band
Royal Gloucestershire Hussars Band
Honourable Artillery Company Band
South Nottinghamshire Hussars (Royal Horse Artillery) Band
Lancashire Artilery Band
34th Northern Signal Regiment Band
Royal Scots Terriorial Band (East Lowlands)
Royal Highland Fusiliers Territorial Band (West Lowlands)
51st Highland Volunteer Band
Princess of Wales's Royal Regiment Territorial Army Band
Warwickshire Band (Territorial Army)
The Volunteer Northumberland Band of the Royal Regiment of Fusiliers

Royal Anglian Territorial Army Band
North West Infantry Band (King's)
Yorkshire Volunteers Band
Devonshire and Dorset Regimental Band (V)
Royal Regiment of Wales Territorial Army Band
Staffordshire Volunteer Band and Bedfordshire and Oxfordshire Band (TA)
The Light Infantry Burma Band (Territorial Army)
150 (Northumbria) Transport Regiment RLC (V) Band
Army Medical Services Territorial Army Band

The Territorial Army (TA)

Currently the TA is restructuring to a strength of 59,000 that would be reinforced in war by Individual Reservists (IRs) to a fully mobilised establishment of 72,000. The TA acts a a General Reserve to the Army, with a secondary but vitally important function being the promotion of a nationwide link between the military and civilian community.

The MoD describes the role of the TA as follows:

a. To reinforce the Regular Army, as and when required, with individuals, subunits and units, either in the UK or overseas;

b. To provide the framework for bringing units up to full War Establishment strength and the basis for forming new units in times of national emergency.

Current plans appear to place a large part of the defence of the mainland UK in the hands of the TA. TA soldiers have been assigned national defence roles such as, guarding vital installations, undertaking reconnaissance and early warning, providing communications and damage control. In early 1995 a composite TA platoon served alongside the regular infantry component of the Falkland Islands garrison, and in Bosnia during late 1996 over 1,200 TA soldiers were serving with the Multi National Division (SW). In the longer term TA Soldiers on short term contracts will almost certainly prove to be a valuable addition to regular units where manpower is at a premium.

TA Infantry Units have a General Pupose structure which will give them flexiblity of employment across the spectrum of military operations. All Infantry Battalions, including Parachute Battalions, have a common establishment of three Rifle Companies and a Headquarters Company. In addition, there are four Fire Support Battalions; each with a Headquarters and two Heavy Weapons Companies. Each company will have Milan, Mortar and Machine Gun Platoons. These battalions will provide operational and training support to all TA Battalions.

In general terms, TA Units hold equipment appropriate to their role. Some items of note are:

One TA Yeomanry Regiment, is equipped with Sabre, to provide medium recce support to the ARRC.

Two TA Field Regiments equipped with FH 70 artillery guns.
One TA Engineer Squadron is equipped with M2 bridging system.
Three TA Signal Regiments are equipped with PTARMIGAN.
One TA AAC Regiment is equipped with Gazelle.
One TA NBC Regiment is equipped with Fuchs.

TA volunteers are paid at Regular Army rates (but with a reduced X Factor of 5%) for every full or part day of training. They receive:

a. One part day's pay for attending duties of two to four hours duration;
b. A whole day's pay for duties of eight hours or longer.

In addition, TA personnel can earn an annual taxfree bounty provided they have been available for callout during the training year, attended a minimum amount of training, have passed certain tests and gained the Commading Officers Certificate of Efficiency.

The annual training commitment to qualify for bounty is:

Independent Units: 27 days including 15 days continuous at camp.
Specialist Units: 19 days including 15 days continuous at camp.

In each case, individuals may attend one or more courses aggregated to at least eight days duration in lieu of camp, with the balance of seven days being carried out in extra out of camp training.

Some examples of bounty payments and commitments are:

Group A (Independent and Specialist Units)

Commitment	Bounty payment on completion of:
1st Year	275
2nd Year	575
3rd and 4th years	850
5th Year	900

TA Callout procedure

Under present legislation, TA Independent and Specialist Units or individuals (together with the Army's IRs) are liable for callout by Queen's Order: 'for service in any part of the world when warlike operations are in preparation or progress' (Reserve Forces Act (RFA) 1980, Sects 11 and 12). 'If national danger is imminent or a great emergency has arisen' they may be called out by Queen's Order for permanent worldwide service under RFA 80 Sect 10. The Secretary of State alone may callout the TA in defence of the United Kingdom or Channel Islands. Ministers undertook, when the TA was restructured in 1967, to callout the TA under Sect 11 only after full use had been made of all suitable members of the Regular Forces (Section A). IR may be called in aid of the Civil Powers to keep the peace.

TA soldiers are calledout using the same procedures as for IRs; ie they are sent a CallOut Notice specifying the time, date and place to which they are to report. If TA Units or SubUnits are calledout, they form up with their vehicles and equipment at their TA Centres or other designated locations. They would then be deployed by land, sea and air to their operational locations in the UK or overseas. However, if TA personnel are calledout as individuals, they would report to a Temporary Mobilisation Centre where they would be processed before posting to reinforce a unit or HQ.

Following a major study of the mix of Regular and Reserve Forces, an Open Government document was published for discussion. The document contains three radical proposals:

a. The introduction of a High Readiness Reserve, members of which would be calledout at the behest of the Secretary of State to reinforce the Regular Army regardless of whether a Queen's Order had been issued or not.

b. The introduction of a new level of callout to allow Volunteer and Regular Reservists to be calledout to assist in humanitarian aid operations, including disaster relief at home and abroad, and UN peacekeeping operations which do not amount to war.

c. The authorization for Reservists to work voluntarily on a full or part time basis with the Regular Forces while remaining in the Reserve Forces.

Having received broad endorsement of these proposals, a further Government document was published in March 1995. This document contained the draft text of the new Reserve Forces Act and a comprehensive explanation of the meaning of each of the clauses of the Act. Comments on this document were consolidated during the Summer of 1995 and the draft Act revised ready for presentation to Parliament in due course.

The Regular Reserve

Individual Reservists (IR): are former members of the Regular Army who after completion of their fulltime service may be recalled to the Colours, or who volunteer after their legal Reserve obligation has expired. They have varying degrees of liability for recall and training depending upon factors such as period of Regular Army service, age and sex. Categories of IR are described below:

a. **The Regular Army Reserve of Officers (RARO):** Retired Regular, Army Emergency Reserve or TA Officers. Those granted Commissions from 1 April 1983 have a compulsory training liability for six years after leaving the Active List. Others may volunteer to train.

b. **The Regular Reserve:** Ex-Regular soldiers (male and female) who have a compulsory training liability (normally for six years after leaving the Colours) or who have volunteered to join it from other categories.

c. **The LongTerm Reserve:** Men (but not women) who have completed their Regular Reserve liability and who serve in this category until aged 45. They have no training liability.

d. **Army Pensioners:** Ex-Regular soldiers (male and female) who are in receipt of a Service pension. They have a legal liability for recall to age 60 (but only to age 55 would be invoked). They have no training liability.

Callout Procedure

IR are required to keep at home an Instruction Booklet (AB 592A), their ID card and a personalised Booklet (AB 592B). The AB 592A provides IR with general instructions on what they have to do if mobilised. It contains a travel warrant and a special cash order. The AB 592A is computer produced and updated quarterly as required, to take account of such changes as address, medical category and age. It explains where the reservist is to report on mobilisation and arrangements for pay and allotments, next of kin, clothing held etc.

Under present legislation, IR may only be mobilised if called out by Queen's Order. Mobilisation may involve only a few individuals/units or any number up to general mobilisation when all are called out. If mobilisation is authorised Notices of CallOut are despatched to those IR concerned by Recorded Delivery as the legal notification. Announcements of callout are also made by the press, radio and television.

The most recent instance of the mobilisation of IR was in the build up to Operation RESOLUTE for the Bosnia IFOR when 52 IR were calledout (joined by 397 members of the TA). During the Gulf War, 503 IR (together with 1,053 members of the TA) were calledout for service. The majority, on that occasion, were medically trained personnel and the remainder were deployed in UK, BAOR and Cyprus to relieve Regular Army personnel for service in the Gulf.

Under the proposals for the new Reserve Forces Act, IR will be liable to callout under the same new provisions as described above for the TA. In addition, the Act will bring the conditions relating to all three Services in line and will include officers and pensioners who are currently covered by separate legislation/Royal Warrants.

Training

Only Regular Reservists and some members of RARO have a liability to train. The legal liability is for up to 15 days plus four periods of 36 hours each year. This liability has not been enforced for many years.

The only training that is currently funded is for 1,500 man/ weeks per year to enable the RARO and Regular Reservists who volunteer to take part in collective training with both Regular and TA Units. Payment is made at TA rates plus a £215 (taxfree) bounty.

The Annual Reporting Exercises (ARCES), which required some RARO and all Regular Reservists to report for one day to have their clothing and documentation checked and undergo a brief 1+ hours training period also ceased in 1991. The reporting element has now been replaced by a postal system which provides a payment of £20 (taxed) to those who return an updated proforma.

Cadets

The Role of the CCF

The Combined Cadet Force (CCF) is a tri-service military cadet organisation based in schools and college throughout the UK. Although it is administered and funded by the Services it is a part of the national youth movement.

The CCF receives assistance and support for its training programme from the Regular and Reserve Forces, but the bulk of adult support is provided by members of school staffs who are responsible to head teachers for the conduct of cadet activities. CCF officers wear uniform but they are not part of the Armed Forces and carry no liability for service or compulsory training.

There are some 240 CCF contingents with 40,000 cadets, of whom some 25,000 are Army Cadets. The role of the CCF is to help boys and girls to develop powers of leadership through training which promotes qualities of responsibility, self-reliance, resourcefulness, endurance, perseverance and a sense of service to the community. Military training is also designed to demonstrate why defence forces are needed, how they function and to stimulate an interest in a career as an officer in the Services.

The Role of the ACF

The role of the Army Cadet Force (ACF) is to inspire young people to achieve success with a spirit of service to the Queen, country and their local community, and to develop the qualities of good citizenship, responsibility and leadership.

There are 1,674 ACF detachments based in communities around the UK with a strength of around 40,000 cadets. The ACF is run by over 7,000 adults drawn from the local community who manage a broad programme of military and adventurous training activities designed to develop character and leadership.

CHAPTER 14 - MISCELLANEOUS

The Military Hierarchy

Rank	Badge	Appointment Example
General (Gen)	Crown, Star & Crossed Sword with Baton	Adjutant General
Lieutenant General (Lt Gen)	Crown & Sword & Baton	Commander ARRC
Major General (Maj Gen)	Star & Sword & Baton	Divisional Commander
Brigadier (Brig)	Crown & 3 Stars	Brigade Commander
Colonel (Col)	Crown & 2 Stars	Staff or School
Lieutenant Colonel (Lt Col)	Crown & 1 Star	Battle Group/ Armoured Regiment/Infantry Bn
Major (Maj)	Crown	Sqn/ Coy/Bty
Captain (Capt)	3 Stars	Squadron/Company 2ic
Lieutenant (Lt)	2 Stars	Troop/Pl Commander
2nd Lieutenant	1 Star (2/Lt)	Troop/Pl Commander
Warrant Officer First Class	Royal Coat of Arms on Forearm	Regimental Sergeant Major (WO 1) (RSM)
Warrant Officer Second Class	Crown on forearm	Company Sergeant Major (WO 2) (CSM)
Staff Sergeant (Ssgt)	Crown over stripes	Coy/Sqn Stores (or Colour Sergeant)
Sergeant (Sgt)	3 stripes	Platoon Sergeant
Corporal (Cpl)	2 stripes	Section Commander
Lance Corporal	1 Stripe	Section 2ic (Lcpl)

Modes of Address

Where appropriate soldiers are addressed by their generic rank without any qualifications, therefore Generals, Lieutenant Generals and Major Generals are all addressed as General. Colonels and Lieutenant Colonels as Colonel, Corporals and Lance Corporals as Corporal. Staff Sergeants and Colour Sergeants are usually addressed as Staff or Colour and CSMs as Sergeant Major. It would almost certainly be prudent to address the RSM as "Sir".

Private Soldiers should always be addressed by their title and then their surname. For example: Rifleman Harris, Private Jones, Bugler Bygrave, Gunner Smith, Guardsman Johnson, Sapper Williams, Trooper White, Kingsman Boddington, Signalman Robinson, Ranger Murphy, Fusilier Ramsbotham , Driver Wheel, Craftsman Grease or Air Trooper Rotor. However, it should be remembered that regiments and corps have different customs and although the above is a reasonable guide it may not always be correct.

Regimental Head-Dress

The normal everyday headdress of NCOs and Soldiers (and in some regiments of all ranks) is the beret or national equivalent. The norm is the dark blue beret. Exceptions are as follows:

a.	Grey Beret	The Royal Scots Dragoon Guards Queen Alexandra's Royal Army Nursing Corps
b.	Brown Beret	The King's Royal Hussars The Royal Wessex Yeomanry
c.	Khaki Beret	All Regiments of Foot Guards The Honourable Artillery Company The Kings Own Royal Border Regiment The Royal Anglian Regiment The Prince of Wales's Own Regiment of Yorkshire The Green Howards The Duke of Wellington's Regiment
d.	Black Beret	The Royal Tank Regiment
e.	Rifle Green Beret	The Light Infantry The Royal Green Jackets The Brigade of Gurkhas Adjutant General's Corps
f.	Maroon Beret	The Parachute Regiment
g.	Beige Beret	The Special Air Service Regiment

h.	Light Blue Beret	The Army Air Corps
i.	Scarlet Beret	Royal Military Police
j.	Cypress Green Beret	The Intelligence Corps

The majority of Scottish Regiments wear the Tam-O-Shanter (TOS) and the Royal Irish Regiment wear the Corbeen.

Regular Army Rates of Pay as at 1st December 1996

Officers	On Appointment	Rising To
University Cadet	8,062	11,344
Second Lieutenant	14,063	-
Lieutenant	18,589	20,545
Captain	23,668	27,521
Major	30,054	36,010
Lieutenant Colonel	42,281	46,734
Colonel	49,147	54,315
Brigadier	60,257	

Notes:
(1) Rates of pay apply to both male and female officers.
(2) QARANC Officers are commissioned as Lieutenants.

Adult Soldiers	Band	Scale A (£ per week)	£ per Annum
Private Class 4	1	168.98	8,811
Private Class 3	1	189.28	9,869
Private Class 3	2	222.05	11,547
Private Class 3	3	254.23	13,220
Private Class 2	1	211.61	11,033
Private Class 2	2	243.00	12,636
Private Class 2	3	276.90	14,399
Private Class 1	1	230.16	12,001
Private Class 1	2	261.51	13,599
Private Class 1	3	295.36	15,359
Lance Corporal Class 1	1	264.46	13,789
Lance Corporal Class 1	2	296.00	15,392
Lance Corporal Class 1	3	329.48	17,133

Corporal Class 1	1	303.66	15,833
Corporal Class 1	2	335.09	17,425
Corporal Class 1	3	371.70	19,330
Sergeant	4	334.60	17,447
Staff Sergeant	5	387.03	20,187
Warrant Officer Class 2	6	456.40	23,801
Warrant Officer Class 1	7	526.89	27,473

Notes:
(1) Pay scales apply to both males and females. (2) These rates only show the most common basic pay rates. (3) From the 1st January 1991 all recruits are enlisted on an Open Engagement. The Open Engagement is for a period of 22 years service from the age of 18 or the date of enlistment whichever is the later. Subject to giving 12 months notice, and any time bar that may be in force, all soldiers have the right to leave on the completion of 3 years reckonable service from the age of 18.

Length of Service Increments (LSI)

Daily Rates - After 9 years service personnel are eligible for extra daily long service increments of pay. These vary according to rank.

Rank	9 yrs	12 yrs	15 yrs	18 yrs	22 yrs
Pte	0.79	1.12	1.12	1.12	1.12
LCpl	0.79	1.12	1.12	1.12	1.12
Cpl	0.79	1.12	1.36	1.36	1.36
Sgt	0.96	1.36	1.68	1.99	1.99
SSgt	0.96	1.36	1.68	2.31	2.31
WO2	0.96	1.36	1.68	2.31	2.64
WO1	0.96	1.36	1.68	2.31	3.03

Soldiers Pay Bands

All employments in the Army are grouped into Bands for calculating pay. Band 1 includes all recruits during training and the majority of employments. In general, the more skilled the employment, the higher the pay band. Examples of Band 2 Employments are Bandsman; Farrier; Driver Tank Transporter; Radar Operator(RA); Command Post Assistant(RA); Meteorologist; OP Assistant(RA); Surveyor(RA); Armoured Engineer; Amphibious Engineer; Bomb Disposal Engineer; Telecom Op (Linguist); Telecom Op (Systems); Student Nurse; Op Theatre Technician; Pharmacy Technician; Dental Technician; Operator Special Intelligence; Armourer, Blacksmith; Bricklayer; Carpenter; Construction Materials Technician; Draughtsman; Driver Specialist(RE); Electrician; Fitter; Gun Fitter; Metalsmith; Painter; Plant Operator; Plumber;Printer; Railwayman, Sheetmetal Worker; Shipwright, Vehicle Electrician; Vehicle Mechanic, Welder; Well Driller.

Examples of Band 3 employments are - Survey Technician; Telecom Op (Telegraph); Laboratory Technician; Physiological Measurement Technician; Registered General Nurse; Registered Mental Nurse; Telecom Op (Special); Telecom Technician; Physiotherapist; Aircraft Technician; Control Equipment Technician; Radar Technician; Marine Engineer; Radiographer; Avionics Technician; Instrument Technician; SAS Soldier.

Junior Entrants

Age	£ per week	£ per annum
16 but under 17 yrs	105.28	5,489
17 but under 17.5 yrs	127.75	6,661
17.5 years and over*	168.98	8,811

*While in apprentice training.

Charges	£ per Week
Standard food charge	21.21

Single Accommodation Charges (Grade 1)

Major and Above	22.89
Captain & Below	22.82
Senior NCO	17.01
Cpl and Below	9.94
Junior Soldiers	7.77

Additional Pay	£ per Week
Parachutists - All ranks	24.50

The Royal Marines

Although the Royal Marines (RM) are an organisation that is part of the Royal Navy, they are trained and equipped for warfare on land, and it is very likely that they could be involved in operations and exercises with Army units. The Royal Marines number approximately 6,500 officers and men and their primary task is the reinforcement of Norway and NATO's Northern Flank, should a threat develop in that area

The Royal Marines also have detachments on 12 ships at sea and a number of smaller units world-wide with widely differing tasks. However, the bulk of the manpower of the Royal Marines is grouped in battalion sized organisations known as Commandos (Cdo). There are 3 Commando Groups and they are part of a larger formation known as 3 Commando Brigade (3 Cdo Bde).

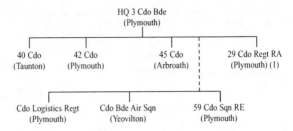

HQ 3 Cdo Bde
(Plymouth)

| 40 Cdo | 42 Cdo | 45 Cdo | 29 Cdo Regt RA |
| (Taunton) | (Plymouth) | (Arbroath) | (Plymouth) (1) |

| Cdo Logistics Regt | Cdo Bde Air Sqn | 59 Cdo Sqn RE |
| (Plymouth) | (Yeovilton) | (Plymouth) |

Note: (1) 29 Cdo Regt RA has one battery stationed at Arbroath with 45 Cdo.

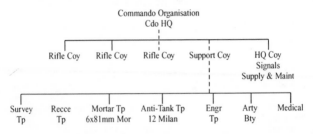

Commando Organisation
Cdo HQ

| Rifle Coy | Rifle Coy | Rifle Coy | Support Coy | HQ Coy Signals Supply & Maint |

| Survey Tp | Recce Tp | Mortar Tp 6x81mm Mor | Anti-Tank Tp 12 Milan | Engr Tp | Arty Bty | Medical |

Note: A troop (Tp) equates to an army platoon. Each rifle company has three troops.

RAF Regiment

Currently the RAF Regiment exists to provide ground and short range air defence for RAF installations, and to train all of the RAF's combatant personnel to enable them to contribute to the defence of their units. During mid 1996, the strength of the RAF Regiment was approximatey 2,400 (including 312 officers).

As of 1 Jan 1997 RAF Regiment units are as follows:

15 Sqn RAF Regt	Honnington	Rapier
16(R) Sqn RAF Regt	Honnington	Rapier
26 Sqn RAF Regt	Laarbruch	Rapier
27 Sqn RAF Regt	Waddington	Rapier
37 Sqn RAF Regt	Bruggen	Rapier
48 Sqn RAF Regt	Lossiemouth	Rapier
1 Sqn RAF Regt	Laarbruch	Field
2 Sqn RAF Regt	Honnington	Field
3 Sqn RAF Regt	Aldergrove	Field

34 Sqn RAF Regt	Leeming	Field
63(QCS) RAF Regt	Uxbridge	Field & Ceremonial
2503 Sqn R Aux AF Regt	Waddington	Field
2620 Sqn R Aux AF Regt	Marham	Field
2623 Sqn R Aux AF Regt	Honnington	Field
2624 Sqn R Aux AF Regt	Brize Norton	Field
2625 Sqn R Aux AF Regt	St Mawgan	Field
4624 (Movs) Sqn R Aux AF Regt	Brize Norton	Movements
4626 (Med) Sqn R Aux AF Regt	Lyneham	Aeromedical

There are now two basic RAF Regiment squadron organisations - the field squadron organised for ground defence against possible enemy ground action and the Rapier squadron organised for defence against low-flying enemy aircraft. There are nine dedicated field squadrons and 63 (QCS) Squadron with a dual ceremonial/field squadron role. Six Rapier squadrons defend RAF airbases in both the UK and Germany.

Rapier Squadron-Possible Organisation

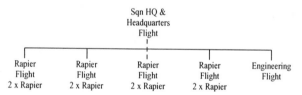

Codewords and Nicknames

A Codeword is a single word used to provide security cover for reference to a particular classified matter, eg Corporate was the Codeword for the recovery of the Falklands in 1982. In 1990 Granby was used to refer to operations in the Gulf and Op Resolute is used for current operations in support of NATO forces in the former Yugoslavia. A Nickname consists of two words and may be used for reference to an unclassified matter, eg Lean Look referred to an investigation into various military organisations in order to identify savings in manpower.

Dates and Timings

When referring to timings the British Army uses the 24 hour clock. This means that 2015 hours, pronounced twenty fifteen hours, is in fact 8.15pm. Soldiers usually avoid midnight and refer to 2359 or 0001 hours. Time zones present plenty of scope for confusion! Exercise and Operational times are expressed in Greenwich Mean Time (GMT) which may differ from the local time. The suffix Z (Zulu) denotes GMT and A (Alpha) GMT + 1 hour. B (Bravo) means GMT + 2 hours and so on.

The Date Time Group or DTG can be seen on military documents and is a point of further confusion for many. Using the military DTG 1030 GMT on 20th April 1997 is written as

201030Z APR 97. When the Army relates days and hours to operations a simple system is used:

a. D Day is the day an operation begins.
b. H Hour is the hour a specific operation begins.
c. Days and hours can be represented by numbers plus or minus of D Day. Therefore if D Day is the 20th April 1997, D-2 is the 18th April and D + 2 is the 22nd April. If H Hour is 0600hrs then H+2 is 0800 hours.

Phonetic Alphabet

To ensure minimum confusion during radio or telephone conversations difficult words or names are spelt out letter by letter using the following NATO standard phonetic alphabet:

ALPHA - BRAVO - CHARLIE - DELTA - ECHO - FOXTROT - GOLF - HOTEL - INDIA - JULIET - KILO - LIMA - MIKE - NOVEMBER - OSCAR - PAPA - QUEBEC - ROMEO - SIERRA - TANGO - UNIFORM - VICTOR - WHISKEY - X RAY - YANKEE - ZULU.

Military Quotations

Young officers and NCOs may find some of these quotations useful on briefings etc; there are two groups Military and General.

Military

"A few honest men are better than numbers."
Oliver Cromwell

"There has to be a beginning to every great undertaking."
Sir Francis Drake

"The beatings will continue until morale improves."
Attributed to the Commander of the Japanese Submarine Force.

"Do the business of the day on the day."
The Duke of Wellington

"Take Risks. A ship in port is safe, but that is not what ships are for. Sail out to sea and do new things."
Rear Admiral Grace Hopper USN (died 1992)

"When other Generals make mistakes their armies are beaten; when I get into a hole, my men pull me out of it."
The Duke of Wellington -after Waterloo

"One might as well try to charge through a wall."
Napoleon On St Helena - Regarding the British
Infantry

"Take short views, hope for the best and trust in God."
Sydney Smith

*"When the violence came, however one hated it, and one came to know how it
damaged one's slightly phoney ideals about how man longed only for goodness
and peace, whereas, actually, he loved fighting and knew he shouldn't.
Hypocrisy is the keystone of civilisation and should be cherished."*
Gerald Hanley - Life & Death Among the Somalis.

*"Nothing is so good for the morale of the troops as occasionally to see a dead
general."*
Field Marshal Slim

*"There is no beating these troops in spite of their generals. I always thought
them bad soldiers, now I am sure of it. I turned their right, pierced their
centre, broke them everywhere; the day was mine, and yet they did not know it
and would not run."*
Marshal Soult - Albuhera 1811

"Confusion in battle is what pain is in childbirth, the natural order of things."
General Maurice Tugwell

"This is the right way to waste money"
PJ O'Rourke Rolling Stone Magazine (Watching
missiles firing during an exercise)

*"This is just something to be got round- like a bit of flak on the way to the
target."*
Group Captain Leonard Cheshire VC - Speaking of
his incurable illness in the week before he died.

*"Pale Ebenezer thought it wrong to fight, But roaring Bill, who killed him,
thought it right."*
Hillare Belloc

"Everyone wants peace - and they will fight the most terrible war to get it."
Miles Kington BBC Radio 4th February 1995

*"The easiest and quickest path into the esteem of traditional military authorities
is by the appeal to the eye rather than to the mind. The polish and pipeclay'
school is not yet extinct, and it is easier for the mediocre intelligence to
become an authority on buttons than on tactics."*
Captain Sir Basil Liddel Hart - Thoughts on War 1944

General

"Whenever I hear about a wave of public idignation I am filled with a massive calm."

Matthew Parris - The Times 24th October 1994

"It is only worthless men who seek to excuse the deterioration of their character by pleading neglect in their early years."

Plutarch - Life of Coriolanus - Approx AD 80

"They say hard work never hurt anybody, but I figured why take the chance."

Ronald Regan

"To applaud as loudly as that for so stupid a proposal means that you are just trying to fill that gap between your ears."

David Starkey BBC (4 Feb 95)

"Its always best on these occasions to do what the mob do." says Mr Pickwick.
"But suppose that there are two mobs?" suggested Mr Snodgrass.
"Shout with the largest" replied Mr Pickwick.

Pickwick Papers Chapter 13

"Don't worry son, we're not expecting too much from you."

Bill Scott Manager of Preston NE to Tom Finney on his debut.

"It is a general popular error to imagine the loudest complainers for the public to be the most anxious for its welfare."

Edmund Burke

"Ah, these diplomats! What chatterboxes! There's only one way to shut them up - cut them down with machine guns. Bulganin, go and get me one!"

Joseph Stalin - As reported by De Gaulle during a long meeting.

"You Liberals think that goats are just sheep from broken homes."

Anon

"I consider myself to be the most important figure in the world."

His Royal Highness - Field Marshal Idi Amin Dada VC.

Abbreviations

The following is a selection from the list of standard military abbreviations and should assist users of this handbook.

AWOL	Absent without leave
accn	Accommodation
ACE	Allied Command Europe
Adjt	Adjutant
admin	Administration
admin O	Administrative Order
ac	Aircraft
AD	Air Defence/Air Dispatch/Army Department
ADA	Air Defended Area
ADP	Automatic Data Processing
AFCENT	Allied Forces Central European Theatre
AIFV	Armoured Infantry Fighting Vehicle
Airmob	Airmobile
ATAF	Allied Tactical Air Force
armr	Armour
armd	Armoured
ACV	Armoured Command Vehicle
AFV	Armoured Fighting Vehicle
AMF(L)	Allied Mobile Force (Land Element)
APC	Armoured Personnel Carrier
APDS	Armour Piercing Discarding Sabot
ARV	Armoured Recovery Vehicle
AVLB	Armoured Vehicle Launched Bridge
AP	Armour Piercing/Ammunition Point/Air Publication
APO	Army Post Office
ARRC	Allied Rapid Reaction Corps
ATGW	Anti Tank Guided Weapon
ATWM	Army Transition to War Measure
arty	Artillery
att	Attached
BE	Belgium (Belgian)
BGHQ	Battlegroup Headquarters
bn	Battalion
bty	Battery
BK	Battery Captain
BC	Battery Commander
BG	Battle Group
bde	Brigade
BAOR	British Army of the Rhine
BFG	British Forces Germany
BFPO	British Forces Post Office
BMH	British Military Hospital
BRSC	British Rear Support Command
C3I	Command, Control, Communications & Intelligence.
cam	Camouflaged
cas	Casualty

CCP	Casualty Collecting Post
CCS	Casualty Clearing Station
CASEVAC	Casualty Evacuation
cat	Catering
CAD	Central Ammunition Depot
CEP	Circular Error Probable/Central Engineer Park
CEPS	Central European Pipeline System
CET	Combat Engineer Tractor
CVD	Central Vehicle Depot
CW	Chemical Warfare
COS	Chief of Staff
civ	Civilian
CP	Close Protection/Command Post
CAP	Combat Air Patrol
c sups	Combat Supplies
CV	Combat Vehicles
CVR(T) or (W)	Combat Vehicle Reconnaissance Tracked or Wheeled
comd	Command/ Commander
CinC	Commander in Chief
CPO	Command Pay Office/Chief Petty Officer
CO	Commanding Officer
coy	Company
CQMS	Company Quartermaster Sergeant
comp rat	Composite Ration (Compo)
COMCEN	Communications Centre
coord	Co-ordinate
CCM	Counter Counter Measure
DAA	Divisional Administrative Area
DTG	Date Time Group
def	Defence
DF	Defensive Fire
DK	Denmark
dml	Demolition
det	Detached
DISTAFF	Directing Staff (DS)
div	Division
DAA	Divisional Administrative Area
DMA	Divisional Maintenance Area
DS	Direct Support/Dressing Station
ech	Echelon
EME	Electrical and Mechanical Engineers
ECCM	Electronic Counter Measure
emb	Embarkation
EDP	Emergency Defence Plan
EMP	Electro Magnetic Pulse
en	Enemy

engr	Engineer
EOD	Explosive Ordnance Disposal
eqpt	Equipment
ETA	Estimated Time of Arrival
EW	Early Warning/Electronic Warfare
ex	Exercise
FRG	Federal Republic of Germany
FGA	Fighter Ground Attack
fol	Follow
fmn	Formation
FUP	Forming Up Point
FAC	Forward Air Controller
FEBA	Forward Edge of the Battle Area
FLET	Forward Location Enemy Troops
FLOT	Forward Location Own Troops
FOO	Forward Observation Officer
FR	France (French)
FRT	Forward Repair Team
FUP	Forming Up Place/Point
GDP	General Defence Plan
GE	German (Germany)
GOC	General Officer Commanding
GPMG	General Purpose Machine Gun
GR	Greece (Greek)
HAC	Honourable Artillery Company
hel	Helicopter
HE	High Explosive
HEAT	High Explosive Anti Tank
HESH	High Explosive Squash Head
HVM	Hyper Velocity Missile
Hy	Heavy
IFF	Identification Friend or Foe
IGB	Inner German Border
II	Image Intensifier
illum	illuminating
IO	Intelligence Officer
INTSUM	Intelligence Summary
IRG	Immediate Replenishment Group
IS	Internal Security
ISD	In Service Date
IT	Italy (Italian)
IW	Individual Weapon
JFHQ	Joint Force Headquarters
JHQ	Joint Headquarters
JSSU	Joint Services Signals Unit
LAD	Light Aid Detachment (REME)

L of C	Lines of Communication
LLAD	Low Level Air Defence
LO	Liaison Officer
Loc	Locating
log	Logistic
LRATGW	Long Range Anti Tank Guided Weapon
LSW	Light Support Weapon
MAOT	Mobile Air Operations Team
MBT	Main Battle Tank
maint	Maintain
mat	Material
med	Medical
mech	Mechanised
MFC	Mortar Fire Controller
MNAD	Multi National Airmobile Division
MO	Medical Officer
MP	Military Police
MOD	Ministry of Defence
mob	Mobilisation
MovO	Movement Order
msl	missile
MV	Military Vigilance
NAAFI	Navy, Army and Air Force Institutes
NADGE	NATO Air Defence Ground Environment
NATO	North Atlantic Treaty Organisation
NCO	Non Commissioned Officer
nec	Necessary
NL	Netherlands
NO	Norway (Norwegian)
NOK	Next of Kin
ni	Night
NORTHAG	Northern Army Group
NTR	Nothing to Report
NBC	Nuclear, Biological and Chemical Warfare
NYK	Not Yet Known
OP	Observation Post
OC	Officer Commanding
OCU	Operational Conversion Unit (RAF)
OIC	Officer in Charge
opO	Operation Order
ORBAT	Order of Battle
pax	Passengers
POL	Petrol, Oil and Lubricants
P info	Public Information
PJHQ	Permanent Joint Head Quarters
Pl	Platoon

PO	Portugal (Portuguese)
QM	Quartermaster
RAP	Rocket Assisted Projectile/Regimental Aid Post
RJDF	Rapid Joint Deployment Force
RTM	Ready to Move
RCZ	Rear Combat Zone
rec	Recovery R & D Research and Development
rebro	Rebroadcast
recce	Reconnaissance
Regt	Regiment
RHQ	Regimental Headquarters
RMA	Rear Maintenance Area/Royal Military Academy
rft	Reinforcement
RSA	Royal School of Artillery
RSME	Royal School of Mechanical Engineering
RTU	Return to Unit
SACUER	Supreme Allied Commander Europe
SATCOM	Satellite Communications
2IC	Second in Command
SH	Support Helicopters
SHAPE	Supreme Headquarters Allied Powers Europe
sit	Situation
SITREP	Situation Report
SIB	Special Investigation Branch
SMG	Sub Machine Gun
SLR	Self Loading Rifle
SMG	Sub Machine Gun
smk	Smoke
SNCO	Senior Non Commissioned Officer
SP	Spain (Spanish)
Sqn	Squadron
SP	Self Propelled/Start Point
SSM	Surface to Surface Missile
SSVC	Services Sound and Vision Corporation
STOL	Short Take Off and Landing
tac	Tactical
tk	Tank
tgt	Target
TOT	Time on Target
TCP	Traffic Control Post
tpt	Transport
tp	Troop
TCV	Troop Carrying Vehicle
TLB	Top Level Nudget
TU	Turkish (Turkey)
TUL	Truck Utility Light

TUM	Truck Utility Medium
UK	United Kingdom
UKMF	United Kingdom Mobile Force
UNCLASS	Unclassified
UXB	Unexploded Bomb
US	United States
U/S	Unserviceable
veh	Vehicle
VOR	Vehicle off the Road
WE	War Establishment
wh	Wheeled
WIMP	Whinging Incompetent Malingering Person
WMR	War Maintenance Reserve
WO	Warrant Officer
wksp	Workshop
X	Crossing (as in roads or rivers)

This publication was produced by R&F (Defence) Publications.
Editorial Office Tel 01743 - 235079
E Mail 101336.3014Compuserve.Com

The other publications in this series are:

The Royal Air Force Pocket Guide 1994-95
The Armed Forces of the United Kingdom 1996-97
The United States Army Guide (Available late 1997)

Further copies can be obtained from:
Pen & Sword Books Ltd
47 Church Street
Barnsley S70 2AS

Telephone: 01226-734222   Fax: 01226-734438

There are special rates for purchases of more than 10 books.

6th Edition March 1997

Photographs: Front Cover by Kevin Harvey of MOD Media Operations and rear cover by
Stuart Bingham of HQ 5 Div Media Operations. Photographs are Crown Copyright.

Would you like to receive information about other
Leo Cooper/Pen & Sword books?

Write for further information to:

Pen & Sword Books Limited
FREEPOST SF5
47 Church Street
BARNSLEY
South Yorkshire S70 2BR

*and receive a colour catalogue containing infor-
mation about our latest publications
or* Telephone 01226 - 734555

SOLDIER TALK
A Squaddies Handbook
SIMON CULLEN, MBE

All of us know the expression 'to swear like a trooper' – but just how does a trooper swear? Not by peppering every sentence with obscenities – far from it, a soldier's language is far more colourful and complicated. The author, Simon Cullen MBE, who served in the Royal Corps of Transport, has heard it all first hand and now provides a hands-on guide to the arcane world of military jargon.

ISBN 0 85052 459 8
240 pages   £6.95

THE ARMED FORCES OF THE UNITED KINGDOM

1996-1997

CHARLES HEYMAN

The Armed Forces of the United Kingdom covers all the vital aspects of the organisations and equipment of the UK Army, Royal Navy and Royal Air Force. Photographs and silhouettes illustrate all major equipment of the three services.

ISBN 0 85052 479 2
248 pages   £9.95

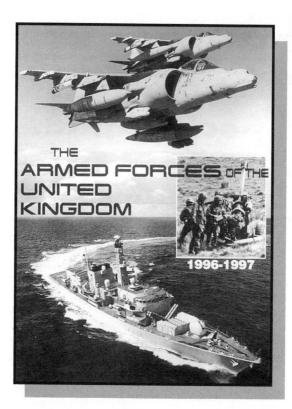

THE
ARMED FORCES OF THE
UNITED
KINGDOM

1996-1997

THE ROYAL AIR FORCE
a pocket guide

Editor CHARLES HEYMAN

A comprehensive pocket guide to the organisation, equipment and tactics of today's Royal Air Force. This is a time when the RAF is being closely looked at in the light of the approaching new century; its requirements, role and future equipment needs being a matter of intense debate.

ISBN 0 85052 416 4
140 pages   £3.95

THE ROYAL AIR FORCE

a pocket guide

There were good reasons why she couldn't escape him....

For one, he held her tight, so tight that to onlookers, his actions must have appeared intimate and caring. But Eden wasn't fooled.

"Listen to me," he said, softly, lovingly, in her ear. "Try to remember. Innocent people die when you're around. If you keep this up, someone else might get hurt."

Eden nodded, clearly seeing Christian Tierney for what he was. Bulletproof. Clever and daring enough to steal her away under the noses of two lawmen and an assassin. Brutal enough to dictate her cooperation. Powerful enough to command a hijacking without ever drawing a weapon.

No matter how much he terrified her, she could never escape him now.

Because he'd saved her life twice in less than three hours.

Dear Reader,

What is it about mysterious men that always makes our pulse race? Whether it's the feeling of risk or the excitement of the unknown, dangerous men have always been a part of our fantasies. And now they're a part of Harlequin Intrigue. Throughout half of 1996, we'll kick off each month with one of our DANGEROUS MEN. This month, meet Christian Tierney in *Reckless Lover* by Carly Bishop.

Romantic suspense is the favorite genre of Denver author Cheryl McGonigle, writing as Carly Bishop. A long-time member of Rocky Mountain Fiction Writers, she won the coveted RMFW Writer of the Year award in 1991. Cheryl finds writing romantic suspense one of life's great joys—in the manner of Joseph Campbell's maxim, Follow your bliss—and she's likely to be doing more of it, as her only daughter is off to college next fall.

With our DANGEROUS MEN promotion, Harlequin Intrigue promises to keep you on the edge of your seat...and the edge of desire.

Regards,

Debra Matteucci
Senior Editor & Editorial Coordinator
Harlequin Books
300 East 42nd Street
New York, NY 10017